OXFORD MEDICAL PUBLICATIONS

Down Syndrome

THE FACTS

Down Syndrome

THE FACTS

Mark Selikowitz
Consultant Paediatrician and Director
Tumbatin Developmental Clinic
The Prince of Wales Children's Hospital
Sydney, Australia

Oxford New York Tokyo
OXFORD UNIVERSITY PRESS
1990

Oxford University Press, Walton Street, Oxford OX2 6DP

Oxford   New York   Toronto
Delhi   Bombay   Calcutta   Madras   Karachi
Petaling Jaya   Singapore   Hong Kong   Tokyo
Nairobi   Dar es Salaam   Cape Town
Melbourne   Auckland
and associated companies in
Berlin   Ibadan

Oxford is a trade mark of Oxford University Press

Published in the United States
by Oxford University Press, New York

© M. Selikowitz 1990

British Library Cataloguing in Publication Data
Selikowitz, Mark
Down syndrome.
1. Man. Down's syndrome I
I. Title
616.85'8842
ISBN 0-19-261872-5
ISBN 0-19-261901-2 (pbk)

Library of Congress Cataloging-in-Publication Data
Selikowitz, Mark.
Down syndrome: the facts/Mark Selikowitz.
(Oxford medical publications)
Includes index.
1. Down's syndrome—Popular works.   I. Title.   II. Series
RJ506.D68S45   1989   618.92'85'8842—dc20   89-15961
ISBN 0-19-261872-5
ISBN 0-19-261901-2 (pbk.)

Set by Graphicraft Typesetters Ltd., Hong Kong
Printed in Great Britain by
Biddles Ltd, Guildford and King's Lynn

Preface

This book has been written for parents who have a child with Down syndrome. It will also be of interest to relatives, friends, teachers, therapists, doctors, and others who come into contact with your child. But it is to you, the parent, that it is primarily directed.

There have been enormous changes for people with Down syndrome over the past two decades. Children with the syndrome now usually live at home and enjoy the love and stimulation they receive from their families. They benefit from early teaching and special help through the school years. Included in everyday activities, they are socially more competent, and their needs for recreation and friendship are increasingly being catered for. With improved health care, they are living healthier lives. For adults, vocational training and employment prospects are increasing, as are opportunities for supervised living in the community. There has also been an expansion in community support services providing help to parents. There is no doubt that parents can now look forward to a brighter future for their child than ever before.

These changes have brought with them new choices, and parents need to be better informed than in the past. With a range of options, and often conflicting advice from different quarters, parents are asking many questions: Should I take my child to early intervention? Does it work? Is one form better than another? How much of the programme should I follow at home? How do I discipline my child? What do I tell my other children? Should I send my child to a pre-school group? Should my child attend a special school or an ordinary school? Special recreation or ordinary recreation programmes? What about my child's sexual development? What special health precautions should be taken? How do I get the most out of services? Who will look after my child when I am no longer able to do so? And many more.

As a developmental paediatrician seeing many children with Down syndrome and their parents, I am aware that there is no single right answer to many of these questions. In the chapters ahead, I shall try to help you make informed decisions for your child and your family.

Although a book cannot take the place of a doctor or other professional with first-hand knowledge of your child, it can still be a great help. Professionals are usually busy people, and so are parents. At a consultation there is often not enough time to ask all your questions, and even when you do, your anxiety may make explanations difficult to follow and hard to remember. Many professionals take a narrow view of the range of challenges you face and have difficulty answering questions outside their field. Some are so committed to a particular treatment that they cannot always remain objective. A book can go a long way to compensate for these deficiencies by allowing you to absorb information at your convenience. It also gives you the opportunity for quick reference and repeated reading.

This book covers the challenges you may face during your child's infancy, childhood, and adulthood. There are chapters on the cause of Down syndrome, antenatal diagnosis, development, health, and education. There are chapters giving advice on behaviour management and coping with the reactions of family members and friends. Chapter 9 describes many different types of services. Chapter 15 discusses a number of controversial treatments.

The material in the book is relevant to most English-speaking countries. Where important differences exist, I have pointed these out.

I have not avoided using scientific terms, because it is useful for parents to be aware of them. In all cases, I have explained the term in the text.

To avoid using the cumbersome 'he or she' when referring to the child or adult with Down syndrome, I have used 'he' in some chapters and 'she' in others. Statements are usually applicable to both sexes except where issues relating to sexuality are discussed.

I have written this book in response to parents' requests for a positive, balanced, and practical guide to bringing up a child with Down syndrome. I hope that you will find it helpful.

Sydney, 1989   MS

Acknowledgements

I am grateful to Mr Marcus Cremonese, Graphic Designer at the Medical Illustration Unit, University of New South Wales Teaching Hospitals, who prepared all the excellent drawings and graphs. Mr Michael Combe and Mr Michael Oakey, from the same unit, provided many of the photographs. The photographs used for Figures 1, 19, 21, and 22 were taken by Mr Combe, and those for Figures 2, 13, and 14 were prepared from family snapshots by Mr Oakey. The photograph used for Figure 20 was taken by Mr David Lefcovitch, of the Community Relations Directorate, New South Wales Department of Education. The karyotypes shown in Figures 9 and 10 were kindly prepared by Dr Moh-Ying Yip and Ms Glenda Mullan, from the Cytogenetics Department, The Prince of Wales Hospital.

I am grateful to those children and adults who are portrayed in this book, as well as to their parents, for permission to publish their photographs.

I am indebted to my colleagues Dr Sheila Hollins, Professor Gillian Turner, Dr Owen Jones, Dr Helen Molony, Mrs Jane Sunman, and Ms Barbara Spode for their advice on individual chapters. In addition, Mrs Jane Sunman and Mrs Naomi Fletcher kindly proof-read the entire manuscript.

My secretary, Mrs Margaret Boyn, cheerfully took on the extra load of typing the initial drafts from my dictation. She, together with Mrs Jenny Smart and Ms Wendy Grice, typed the final manuscript with great accuracy and speed.

I am also grateful to the many people who provided me with information about services for people with Down syndrome in their respective countries.

One of the pleasures of writing this book has been the support I have received from the staff of the Oxford University Press.

Finally, I thank my wife, Jill, for her advice and encouragement. This book is dedicated to her and to our children, Daniel and Anne, with love.

Contents

1. The first days are the hardest   1
2. Coping with family and friends   13
3. What is Down syndrome?   26
4. How Down syndrome comes about   33
5. Your child's development   43
6. Your child's health   67
7. The heart   88
8. Your child's behaviour   96
9. A guide to services   108
10. Assessment   115
11. Early intervention and pre-school groups   125
12. Which school?   137
13. Adolescence   146
14. Adulthood   158
15. Controversial treatments   180
16. Future pregnancies   188
    Conclusion   198
    Appendix: Useful addresses   199
    Index   201

1. The first days are the hardest

Most parents react with shock and dismay on hearing that their new-born baby has Down syndrome. No matter how well parents may learn to cope with their child's condition in the years to come, almost all find the initial period very difficult. Parents use words like 'shattered', 'devastated', and 'shocked' to describe their reactions. Some feel that they are losing their sanity, others that their world has come to an end. For nearly all, it is a time of turmoil and sadness.

A BAD TIME FOR BAD NEWS

Down syndrome is one of the few conditions associated with intellectual disability where the diagnosis can be made shortly after birth. Most parents of children with other causes of intellectual disability are spared the difficult period after the birth that parents of children with Down syndrome experience. The former have a chance to get to know their child before the realization that he is not developing as he should dawns upon them, usually during late infancy or the toddler years.

During the period just after your child is born, there are many factors that make it a particularly difficult time to cope with bad news. Let us look at these.

Expectations

When a woman is pregnant, she is said to be 'expecting' a baby. During the pregnancy, most parents are, in fact, expecting a normal child. Surveys have shown that parents often have an unrealistically idealized picture of the child who is to be born. At the end of nine months of expectation, the birth of any child requires some adjustment.

Labour

'Labour' is a descriptive term for the extremely hard physical and emotional task of bringing a baby into the world. The combination of pain, lack of sleep, and nervous tension means that you usually need days to recover after the labour. You are likely to be in poor shape for some time, making it very difficult to cope with the news that your child is different.

Confinement

The process of giving birth used to be described as 'confinement'. Even today mothers are isolated in hospital wards away from family, friends, and distractions. Under these circumstances it is very difficult to keep a sense of perspective and cope with difficulties. Women who have given birth in maternity hospitals are treated in many ways as if they are ill. Observations are made, meals brought round, medicines administered, and visiting often curtailed. All this is done with the aim of helping the mother recover; but it is not surprising that, treated in this way, she may start to feel ill and helpless.

Post-natal 'blues'

To make matters worse, the birth of a baby causes a sudden change in the hormonal environment within a woman's body. The high level of certain hormones present during pregnancy drops suddenly, causing a change in her emotional state. Post-natal 'blues' probably affect all women to some degree, making it even more difficult to cope with disappointment at this time.

You do not yet know your child

Perhaps the most difficult factor for parents who find out that their new-born baby has Down syndrome, is that they do not yet know their child. As one mother said,

When she was born she felt like a stranger. The only thing I knew about her was that she had Down syndrome and that was all I could think of. Now that she is older, I think of her differently. She is my daughter, Jane, with all her individual characteristics. Only some of these are related to the fact that she has Down syndrome.

HOW YOU ARE TOLD IS IMPORTANT

Parents usually find out that their child has Down syndrome at a time when they are particularly vulnerable. Unfortunately, things are often made more difficult because of the way in which they are informed of the diagnosis. While there is no ideal way of being told, some ways are definitely better than others. Research has shown that most parents prefer to be told as soon as possible, that they want to be told together, and that they prefer to have the baby present at the time.

Many parents have expressed dissatisfaction about the way in which they were first told of the diagnosis. Often one parent was told alone, and expected to tell the other. Parents complain of being dealt with in an off-hand manner, of lack of privacy when being informed, and of not being given enough time to ask questions.

There is growing awareness among doctors of the inappropriate way in which many parents are told of their child's diagnosis, and an attempt is being made to educate medical students and practitioners to become more competent in this regard. This is of little comfort, however, to the parents who still feel hurt many years later about the inadequate way things were handled during their time of distress.

WHAT YOU ARE TOLD

It is not only the manner of telling, but also what parents are told that causes later dissatisfaction. Down syndrome is relatively uncommon, and many doctors have limited knowledge and experience of the condition. This means that parents are often given an unrealistically negative picture of Down syndrome, based on out-of-date and inappropriate information.

It is impossible to give parents an accurate picture of what their child will be like, since children with Down syndrome vary so much. A balance between being too pessimistic on the one hand, and raising false hopes on the other, is very difficult to achieve. Long lists of potential problems are likely to be misleading. As one father said,

When my eldest [normal] child was born, no one gave me a list of all the possible things that could happen, like motor-car accidents, meningitis, and the like. In fact, he did break his leg in a motor-car accident and caught meningitis when he was five! When Elsie was born, because she had Down syndrome, the doctor listed all the possible problems. She has never had a day's illness in her life, but, of course, once the problems have been mentioned, it is hard to put them out of your mind.

THE REACTIONS OF PARENTS

Although all parents react slightly differently to the news that their child has Down syndrome, most share some common feelings. They are ordinary people reacting to an extraordinary situation. Reactions usually come from the heart, not the head, and no matter what you know or are told, you may experience feelings that surprise and even frighten you.

I shall describe some of the more common feelings that parents experience after hearing that their child has Down syndrome. Parents often find it helpful to know that others have felt the same way. Even though you may not have experienced these precise emotions, your partner or those around you may have, and it is helpful to recognize them, in order to understand and support one another. Some people feel one particular emotion very strongly, and this may endure for some time. Others experience conflicting emotions.

Shock

This shock reaction was described by a father who told me,

When the doctor mentioned the diagnosis, I felt numb all over. I saw the doctor's mouth open and close, but the only words I heard were 'Down syndrome' and 'retardation'.

All parents go through this phase, even if only for a short period immediately after hearing that their child has Down syndrome. Much of the feeling of shock is experienced physically, and you may feel yourself going cold or perspiring. You may feel nauseated, close to fainting, or experience an overwhelming desire to run away. The shock reaction makes it impossible for you to listen to, and understand, what the doctor is telling you. Do not hesitate to ask him or her to repeat everything again. Always try to check on things that you have heard while in a state of shock, because it is common only to hear isolated phrases, which could give you the wrong impression.

Feeling of disbelief

I kept thinking it was a dream, it was because of the anaesthesia, and that I was going to wake up soon.

When confronted with bad news, one of our most effective protective mechanisms is denial. It is probably necessary to shut our minds, to some degree, in order to cope with a frightening situation. But this sort of disbelief is often total in the initial stage of being told, and parents may feel that their child looks normal and that the doctor is making a mistake.

Once the diagnosis of Down syndrome is confirmed by the chromosome test, most parents are forced to accept that their child has the syndrome. Sometimes, denial may persist in a less obvious way, causing parents to seek many opinions, or become involved in controversial treatments for their child.

Feeling of sorrow

The only other time I felt like I did then was when my father died. It's like a death, it's worse than a death, because the difficulties aren't over. I couldn't hide away and cry like I did when I lost my father, my baby was still there and he needed me.

The reaction to the news that a child has Down syndrome is often likened to the grief felt after the loss of a loved one. In some ways, parents are mourning the loss of the child that they had hoped to have, and this may not be made any easier by the demands made on them by their new baby.

You need opportunities to express your grief. Try to refuse offers of tranquillizers at this time. They do not help you to come to terms with your sadness, and can, in the long run, cause more problems.

Feeling of protectiveness

I kept on going to check whether she was still breathing. I wasn't like that with any of my other children. Eventually, I realized I was becoming over-anxious and I forced myself to stay away for longer and longer periods. With time I calmed down, although I am still more protective of her than I am of the others.

The feeling of protectiveness is a basic instinctive response. While it is a normal and healthy feeling, you will, with time, need to guard against being so protective of your child that he is unable to develop to the best of his ability. It can also be very wearying for you, and can interfere with family life if taken to extremes.

Feeling of revulsion

At first, I couldn't bring myself to touch her at the maternity
hospital. It was only on the third day that I overcame my feelings
and went into the nursery on my own and picked her up.

Although many parents feel embarrassed about mentioning it, a
feeling of revulsion is common during the initial stages. This,
too, is an instinctive response, and probably arose in earlier
times, when a child that was different in any way could not be
properly cared for in a primitive society. Being such a primitive
response, it may be strongly felt. Babies with Down syndrome
are just as appealing as other babies, and most parents find
that such feelings disappear with increasing contact, as the
child becomes more responsive and a bond slowly develops.
The bond between parent and child is not something that
happens suddenly. It is a slow process that continues to develop throughout childhood. You will need to give it time.

Feelings of inadequacy and embarrassment

I felt that I had let everyone down. My husband, my parents, and
my other children. I couldn't bear to face them.

For many parents, the birth of a child with Down syndrome is
a tremendous blow to their self-esteem. They feel that having
given birth to a child with a disability reflects badly on them.
This is particularly so when they do not already have other
children.
    This feeling also gives rise to a feeling of embarrassment and
a tendency to stay away from others.

Everywhere I went, I always thought that people were looking at
him. I used to pull a hat down over his ears and lie him face down
in the pram so that people couldn't see him.

Feeling of anger

I got so angry with the social worker, I said, 'It's all right for you
to talk, both your children are normal'.

Many people feel very angry when they find themselves in a
situation which they cannot change. Anger may be directed

against the doctors, the nursing staff, or family and friends. Anger is a biological reaction. In some situations, it gives us the energy to fight our way out of trouble. Unfortunately, while anger might help parents to assert themselves in the face of adversity, it is generally not a very constructive feeling in this situation.

If anger is directed towards oneself, it may result in depression. Many parents experience this as a feeling of hopelessness and pessimism. They cry readily, sleep and eat poorly, and have no energy or enthusiasm for anything.

Guilt

I felt that I must have done something terribly bad to be punished like this.

Mothers often feel guilty about having a child with Down syndrome, because they are the ones who carry the child during pregnancy. Often, little things that were done, or not done, during the pregnancy loom large in parents' minds.

It is important to realize that the chromosomal error causing Down syndrome occurs prior to conception, and that events during pregnancy play no part.

In the rare case where one of the parents is a carrier, there is still no reason to apportion blame. Every person carries at least two potentially harmful genes, and no one can be held responsible for his or her genetic make-up. Genes, good and bad, are passed from generation to generation in a way that is beyond our control.

MOST PARENTS DO COPE

Once over the initial period, the majority of parents cope well with the special challenges of bringing up their child. Most parents report great pleasure in each new skill their child achieves, and feel that their child is more capable than they had expected. Most find that their child's temperament and behaviour do not present significant problems. Parents also generally report that their child with Down syndrome is healthier than they had anticipated.

WAYS OF COPING

Every parent will find his or her own way of coming to terms with the feelings and difficulties of the period after the diagnosis has been made. Although there is no simple prescription for quick and painless adjustment to the fact that your child has Down syndrome, here is some advice which you may find helpful.

Time is the greatest healer

At the time of your initial distress, it may seem to you that you will never come to terms with your child's condition. Experience has shown that, with the passage of time, parents do adjust to a remarkable degree. With time, intense feelings subside, things are seen in perspective, and you often find strength in yourself and those around you that you were unaware of.

One of the greatest factors in this regard is your child himself. As children with Down syndrome get beyond the first few months, they become more responsive and winning in their ways. With the first responsive smile at about two or three months, many parents report that their attitude to their baby changes. Try to enjoy the things your baby learns to do, and you will find much to delight and reward you.

Be open about the way you feel

Try not to 'bottle up' your feelings. The best way to cope with the intense emotions you feel is to talk about them to others. Do not be afraid to cry and to share your frustrations. There is no better way to diminish distressing feelings than sharing them with a sympathetic friend.

Some parents, particularly fathers, find this very difficult. Many men feel that they have to be 'the strong one', putting themselves under great strain, without allowing emotional release. As one mother told me,

'When my child was born, my husband didn't want to talk about our child or my feelings about her at all. I felt that he was cold and unfeeling. It was only years later that a good friend of ours mentioned that my husband used to sit in the pub every evening and unburden himself. At that time I felt so lonely, I wish he had spoken to me.'

Find a professional you can talk to

Many parents find it a great help if they have someone, such as a social worker, community nurse, or doctor, with whom they can share their feelings. Such a person needs to be able to accept your feelings at this time and not try to cheer you up in an unrealistic way. He or she will also understand that your feelings change, and be able to accept that you feel differently from one day to the next.

A professional such as this can also give helpful information about Down syndrome and any appropriate services available. He or she will be able to bring up subjects that you have not thought of or may be too distressed to raise. This is important, because parents may not know which questions to ask. A father of a child with Down syndrome told me that when his child was born, he was under the impression that children with Down syndrome were ineducable, and therefore did not ask about schooling.

Meet with other parents

Meeting other parents of children with Down syndrome is often a very rewarding experience. There are different ways in which this can be arranged. You may want to meet the parents of an older child with Down syndrome who have already resolved many of the issues that trouble you. In this way, you can find out about their experience and meet their child. While this is helpful for some parents, it can present difficulties. Children with Down syndrome are all different, and, at a time when you are so uncertain about your own child, it is easy to imagine that your child will be exactly like the child you meet. If you do encounter another child with Down syndrome, try to remember that he or she represents just one of many possibilities.

It is also sometimes helpful to be introduced to a couple who have a child the same age as yours. This allows you to share your experiences and feel less isolated. Such friendships often endure as the children grow up.

A way of meeting a number of parents is to attend a parents' group. This is particularly useful for fathers who often do not have the opportunity to come across other parents at play-

groups and early intervention sessions. Although many men are
initially reluctant to attend groups, most find that talking with
other parents who have gone through the same experiences and
have similar feelings can be very helpful.

Get back into society

For one year we didn't go out. Whenever we were invited, we
made some excuse, but really it was because we were afraid to face
people. Eventually, there was a family wedding which we felt we
couldn't miss. With great reluctance, I asked a neighbour if she
would baby-sit and she agreed. We were very apprehensive about
going, but we had the most wonderful time. Everyone said how
pleased they were to see us, and we came home feeling on top of
the world.

Feelings of embarrassment or protectiveness make many parents stay away from others in the period after their baby is
born. Even though it is difficult at first, do try to get out and
about and resume as normal a life as possible. Most people will
be very pleased to have you around again, and normal social
interactions are much easier if there is no hesitancy or delay on
your part.

In the next chapter, I shall discuss the reactions of family and
friends to the news that your child has Down syndrome. To a
large extent, others will take their lead from you, and if you
treat your child as part of your family and society, they usually
will too.

Keep active

Keeping busy is a very good way of overcoming problems for
many parents. I do not mean the frantic sort of busyness that
gives you no repose. Rather, try to have constructive and
satisfying things to do, instead of many idle moments when
worries can loom large.

Many parents find that early intervention programmes provide them with encouragement, support, and constructive
things to do. As one mother put it,

If it had not been for the intervention programme, I would have
gone out of my mind. I now realize that I did too much, but in a
way I needed to. It was important for me to get out and keep busy
while I was recovering from the shock.

Recreational activities you were involved in before your baby was born should be resumed if possible. This is not always easy with a young baby; but if baby-sitting arrangements can be made, do try to find some recreational outlet.

I went to pottery classes one night a week while my husband looked after the baby. I had not been to them since before we were married. It was wonderful. While working with the clay, I didn't have time to think of anything else. I felt so relaxed when I came home, nothing was too much trouble. You can't feel normal if you don't do normal things.

Try to take one step at a time

Parents of children with Down syndrome have so many questions. It is not unusual for parents of babies with Down syndrome to ask me about their child's schooling, employment, and even sexuality and married life. If you can, try to take one day at a time. There is not much point planning for your child too far ahead, as your child, you, and the options available to you, will change with time.

Do not expect total acceptance

Most parents adjust to the fact that their child has Down syndrome, and cope well in the years to come. Yet there are times when feelings of sadness do return, although not with the same intensity and duration as in the first weeks. Some periods are more difficult than others. It may be related to landmark events, such as when your child first goes to school or reaches puberty. Often, it is difficult to know why some of the old sadness returns.

I thought that it was over and that I had come to terms with Margaret having Down syndrome. Then I met a woman who was at the maternity hospital when I gave birth to Margaret. Suddenly, all those feelings came back again. You think you are on top of it, but the wound is still there.

IF YOU DECIDE THAT YOU CANNOT TAKE YOUR BABY HOME

In the past, the minority of babies with Down syndrome were taken home. Now the majority grow up as part of a family.

Nevertheless, there are a small number of parents who feel, often for reasons they cannot explain, that they are unable to take their baby home with them. For such parents, a period of separation from the baby may be needed to reasssess their feelings. Some then return to take their baby home with them. Others continue to feel that having their baby live at home is something that they cannot face. If you feel this way; you will need to talk to someone, such as a social worker or psychologist, who has special skills in helping you come to terms with this difficult decision. You will need to look into the options available, in order to provide the best possible substitute for your own care. Foster-care of children with Down syndrome is now often available. A number of children with Down syndrome have also been successfully adopted.

2. Coping with family and friends

While trying to cope with your own reactions to the birth of your child, you will probably wonder what effect having a child with Down syndrome will have on your marriage, other children, relatives, and friends.

YOUR MARRIAGE

The relationship between parents is one of the most important factors influencing how both they and their children will adjust to life's challenges. The birth of any child can increase tensions in a marriage, and the birth of a child with Down syndrome will always place extra stress on the parents. There have been a number of studies to determine whether the rate of marital disharmony is higher among parents who have a child with Down syndrome. These have shown that this is not the case. The stress of having a child with Down syndrome is not likely to upset a good partnership. In fact, many parents report that their child brought them closer together. The rate of divorce and separation is no higher among parents who have a child with Down syndrome; and this suggests that, if a marriage does fail, the child is unlikely to be the only cause.

How to succeed as partners

Every marriage is a unique partnership, and it is impossible to give specific advice on coping with the challenges a child with Down syndrome may impose upon it. But Tolstoy's comment that 'all happy families are alike' has some truth in it. Certain ingredients seem to be essential for a relationship that will allow personal satisfaction for each of the partners, while at the same time providing an environment in which children can develop and flourish. The most successful partnerships seem to be those in which parents are prepared to share their feelings, support one another through difficult times, and try to arrange things so that they spend time together. Mutual trust and the

Fig. 1. Sophie, aged 15 months, with her family.

ability to compromise over some issues are also necessary for marital harmony.

Husband and wife must be able to talk openly to one another about both happy and sad feelings. It is unlikely that both you and your partner will respond in exactly the same way during the process of coming to terms with your child's problems. Try to understand one another and talk about your feelings in an open way. Hiding your feelings results in misunderstandings and increased tensions. Often one partner, more commonly the wife, will prefer to talk about her concerns, while the other partner may feel that he or she copes best by not discussing them. In such situations it is best to discuss anxieties openly. Such discussions often result in a release of tension and constructive problem-solving, even for the partner who did not initially wish to discuss his or her feelings.

When you feel differently about an issue, try to make use of your differences if possible. One of you may be thinking about the family as a whole, the other of the special needs of the child. One may be making a subjective judgement, the other may be more objective. In most situations, there is more than one way of looking at things; and by taking different attitudes into account, you may eventually come to the best possible decision for everyone concerned. Of course, you will not be able to decide upon everything unanimously. Surveys have shown that most parents do not reach total agreement on about one-third of issues. In such a case it will be necessary for one of you to compromise. In some families, the opinion of one of the parents may tend to prevail in most situations. This is not necessarily bad, provided that the other parent is agreeable.

Marriage is more flexible now than in the past. The roles of partners tend to overlap. Women often need to go out to work, not just for financial reasons, but for self-fulfilment. Fathers are now playing a greater part in the direct care of their children, and many are deriving great satisfaction from this new role. Both partners should share the responsibility of caring for the child with Down syndrome. You should both try to attend doctor's appointments, assessments, and school meetings, and take an active role in decision-making. The tasks undertaken by each partner should be dictated by preference and convenience, rather than by stereotypic models.

In the last chapter, I discussed how important it was for parents to try to get out and about, and to keep active during the early difficult period. It is also important for both partners to make certain that they spend time together during the years while the children are growing up. Children make great demands upon parents' time, and it is important to use baby-sitting, respite-care, and other services to ensure that you have time away from the children to be with one another. There is great emphasis on the development of children with Down syndrome in intervention programmes and schools. Parents, too, need to develop, both individually and in their relationship with one another. All too often this is neglected in efforts to help the child. Children will develop best in a family where their parents have some time for themselves and one another.

All marriages have some degree of conflict, which can usually be resolved by the partners themselves. In situations where this is not possible, it is best to seek professional help from a counsellor skilled in marriage guidance. It is unfortunate that some couples carry on in a state of conflict without resolving it one way or the other. Research has clearly shown that it is family discord that occurs before a separation or divorce, rather than the separation or divorce itself, that is harmful to the development of children.

An increasing number of children are being brought up in single-parent families. In this situation, relatives and friends may need to be called upon to provide extra support. If you are a single parent, you should make certain that you have a professional who can provide you with advice and put you in touch with appropriate services. Often, services such as pre-school centres and respite-care cottages give priority to single parents, and you should take advantage of this. You should also enquire about any special benefits available from government agencies for single parents.

YOUR OTHER CHILDREN

Most children respond well to being the brother or sister of a child with Down syndrome. Strong bonds often develop, and there is even some evidence that siblings of children with Down syndrome are socially more competent and considerate than other children. Research has shown that where emotional stress does occur, it is most commonly experienced by the child born just before or just after the child with Down syndrome.

You may be told or have read that a baby with Down syndrome should be placed in an institution to protect the siblings from emotional stress. But siblings usually identify with their brother or sister with Down syndrome, and often feel great regret and guilt later, if their brother or sister was not able to be part of the family.

It is important for parents to be aware of the problems that siblings of a child with Down syndrome may face, and to take steps to minimize these. Siblings need to understand the nature of Down syndrome, receive attention of their own from parents, cope with the comments and attitudes of other children, and be reassured that they will not have to care for the child with Down syndrome once their parents are no longer able to do so.

They will follow your lead

From the very beginning, your children will be guided by your response to the new baby with Down syndrome. If you bring

Fig. 2. Robbie, aged four, with older sister, Julianne.

the baby home, include her in family activities, and enjoy her achievements, your other children are likely to adjust well. It is important to set the tone from the outset, when you first tell siblings about their new brother or sister with Down syndrome.

Explaining Down syndrome to siblings

1. The sibling under three years

Children under the age of three years are still too young to understand about Down syndrome. But they are often very sensitive to their parents' distress. Do not expect to be able to hide your feelings from your child completely. Young children usually overhear conversations with relatives, and often know that something is amiss. At this age, a child may think that he is the cause of his parents' distress. Although you cannot expect the child to understand about Down syndrome, you will need to explain that you are feeling sad at this time. You will also need to make allowances for difficult behaviour from the child. This may take the form of 'clinging' to a parent, tantrums, or disruptive and attention-seeking behaviour, all to a greater degree than would be expected after the birth of an ordinary baby.

2. The sibling from three to twelve years

After the age of about three years, children need some explanation of Down syndrome, so that it becomes an understandable and accepted part of family life.

When you tell your child about his or her sibling with Down syndrome, try to make certain that both parents are present. This is much easier for all concerned, and allows it to be a family experience, without the feeling that one parent is excluded. It is also a good idea to have the baby with Down syndrome present, preferably held by one of the parents, so that she is treated as a real and valued individual.

For a child under the age of about twelve years, the explanation does not have to be detailed. Try to use simple terms which the child will be able to use himself, when his own friends ask him about his sibling. Do not describe Down syndrome as an illness, as the sibling may become confused. Such an explanation may lead to expectations that a medicine might make the child better again, or that this is something that could be caught, like an infectious disease. It is not useful to use euphemistic terms, such as 'different'. This only leads to confusion, since everybody is 'different' in some way; and it is not an explanation that is likely to satisfy the sibling's friends when they ask questions. The terms 'Down syndrome' and 'handicap' are useful. Most children have a concept of handicap, usually in terms of a physical handicap, and you can explain that there are other types of handicap which affect a wide range of abilities. Children usually understand that a handicap is not something that goes away. Most children between the ages of three and twelve will accept these explanations.

3. The sibling over twelve years

After the age of twelve years, children are more likely to respond with some of the same feelings that parents themselves experience when told of the diagnosis. These were described in the previous chapter. Teenagers and adult siblings will want more detailed information, and may find books such as this one interesting to read. They may also have questions about whether they could have a child with Down syndrome, and may need to be given the opportunity to speak to a geneticist.

The responsibilities of a sibling

With all children over the age of about four or five, it is particularly important to make certain that you do not give them the impression that they will have sole responsibility for the child with Down syndrome when you are no longer able to care for her. You should reassure them that services are available for this purpose. This is a difficult issue for children, who may have ambivalent feelings about caring for their sibling. On the one hand, they may feel that they do not want to be left with the responsibility of looking after a brother or sister with Down syndrome; while on the other hand, they will tend to identify with him or her whenever any care away from home is planned.

You should also try not to put brothers and sisters in a position of having to spend too much time looking after the child with Down syndrome. They do need to have some responsibility; but it should be little more than you would expect from the sibling of a normal child.

Spend special time with all your children

Share your time between all your children. It is important that siblings have some special time with their parents, away from the child with Down syndrome. Special time does not necessarily mean that you have to organize activities away from home. It is time when you are able to give attention to your other children in a way that builds up their self-esteem. The important thing is that it should be enjoyable for the child, and that he or she should be receiving your full attention.

Regular respite-care for the child with Down syndrome is often the best way of ensuring that siblings do get special time with you. This is discussed further in Chapter 9.

Fit the child into your routine

Whenever possible, you should try to get your child with Down syndrome to adapt to your usual routine and be included in family activities. If she cannot be included, it may be better to try to make an alternative arrangement for her, rather than cancel something that is important to the rest of the family. The child with Down syndrome should never become the focus of family life.

The younger sibling

Children who are born after the child with Down syndrome may feel guilty about overtaking their older sibling. Do not make the error of feeling that you should not praise the younger child because this will in some way upset the older. While not in any way trying to compare them, make certain that the younger child is made to feel good about his or her abilities.

Be fair

Make certain you do not spoil the child with Down syndrome, as this can create jealousy in the siblings. Even though the child with Down syndrome may not be as capable, there should still be tasks which she is expected to perform. If one child is expected to make his bed, and the child with Down syndrome is not quite able to do this, she could be expected to play her part with some help from you. This is also beneficial to the child, as it develops independence and builds up self-esteem.

Helping a sibling who is being teased

If a sibling is being teased about his brother or sister with Down syndrome, you will need to give him ways of coping with this. The most important thing is to listen sympathetically. Allow him to express his anger and resentment. If you encourage him to express such feelings to you, they are less likely to build up inside him, or be directed towards the child with Down syndrome. Try also to help him understand the ignorance that is usually behind such teasing.

It is often difficult for a sibling to ignore unkind comments from his peers. It may help your child to imagine that he has a 'magic force-field' surrounding his body which deflects any insults before they can get to him. In this age of science-fiction videos and movies, this idea often appeals to school-aged children.

Others ways of helping siblings are with books and sibling groups, and by enlisting the help of the class teacher.

1. Books for siblings

A number of excellent books* have been written for siblings of children with a handicap. These help siblings know that their problems are not unique, and allow some expression of their feelings. The best books are those that acknowledge the frustrations that siblings feel from time to time.

2. Sibling groups

Groups for siblings of children with disabilities are often organized by one of the services for the intellectually disabled. They usually run for a number of weeks, and children are grouped according to age. Such groups give the children a chance to share experiences, and allow mutual support and friendships to develop. The groups are usually supervised by a trained professional, and the siblings invariably benefit tremendously. For younger children, issues are handled in a simple way. With older children, there is scope for more detailed information to be given, as well as group discussion. One of the strengths of these groups is that children often find it easier to speak about their concerns to their peers. They usually find it difficult to talk about these feelings to their parents, for fear of upsetting them.

3. Involving the class teacher

If a sibling is being teased at school, it may be worth while speaking to his class teacher. The teacher may initiate a discussion about disability in class. When this happens, it is not uncommon for attitudes to disability to change, and having a brother or sister with Down syndrome may be seen as 'special'.

---

* Our brother has Down's syndrome, Cairo, S. (Annick Press), 'Ben', Shennan, V. (The Bodley Head), 'My brother Steven is retarded', Sobol, H. L. (Victor Gollancz).

It may also become apparent during such discussions that there is more than one child in the class who has a sibling with a disability, and this can be very helpful in providing mutual support.

YOUR OWN PARENTS

You will need to tell your own parents that their grandchild has Down syndrome as early as possible. Once more, if possible, you should both be present, and it is better if the baby is held by one of the parents at the time. Your parents' response will probably be similar to that described in the previous chapter. Like you, they will need to be told in a balanced way, and given an opportunity to express their feelings.

Grandparents often feel particularly guilty about a grand-child with Down syndrome, in the mistaken belief that they are in some way responsible for any genetic problem that occurs in the family. You will need to explain to them that this is not the case. They often also have outdated ideas about Down syn-drome, and it is useful if they can be given some up-to-date literature to read.

Occasionally, grandparents will accept information that comes from professionals, while they are more doubtful about what their own children tell them. It may be worth while arranging for them to attend appointments with professionals such as your social worker, doctor, or assessment team.

Try to involve them

It seemed so strange, nothing like this had ever happened in our family. I did not know what to do. When my daughter asked if I would take James to therapy, I was so pleased to be able to do something to help.

Grandparents usually feel very helpless, and it is often best to involve them in some way, so that they have a part to play. They can be an enormous help, baby-sitting, taking a child to intervention, and helping with siblings.

Keep communication open

It is best to be open with your own parents from the very outset. If their attitude upsets or frustrates you, try to explain this to them in a frank manner. Make certain that they do not commit the common error of giving too much attention to the child with Down syndrome, at the expense of your other children. It is very difficult for them to find the right balance, and you may need to guide them.

YOUR OTHER RELATIVES AND FRIENDS

Try to tell your other relatives and friends about your child as early as possible. This usually falls to the father, who is expected to let relatives and friends know once the baby is born. It is better if you do not put off this difficult task, as it then becomes more difficult. Once you have told everyone, you will probably feel a great sense of relief.

Most of the people you tell will feel very uncomfortable, and not know how to respond. To a large degree, they will look to you to provide them with the example of what attitude to take. They may not understand what you are feeling, and may even say totally inappropriate things to you in a well-meaning way. Try to realize that their motives are often good, but that they are hampered by ignorance and out-of-date attitudes. Although you yourself are going through a very difficult period, try not to be too easily discouraged. People can and do change their attitudes, provided that you give them the time to do so. It is worth while realizing that, surprising as it may seem, you may be feeling more comfortable about the situation than they are.

Let her be seen

Whenever possible, let your child with Down syndrome be seen. If people do not see your child they will often imagine that she looks very abnormal, is very sick, or that you cannot cope with her. Friends are invariably very relieved and pleasantly surprised when they actually see how appealing children with Down syndrome are. Once they have seen the child for themselves, many of their fears and awkward feelings decrease, and things become easier for everyone. As one mother told me,

I was worried that people would recoil in horror if I took her out. I dreaded the reaction of the first woman who peered into the pram. I quickly said, 'She's got Down syndrome.' The woman said, 'She's a dear little thing just the same.' I was so pleased. Generally, people are very kind and positive.

Involve your relatives and friends if possible

Friends wanted so much to help. They seemed so grateful if we let them do something. My friend kept offering to look after David, but I did not feel that I should impose on her. Then one day I was sick, and asked her to mind him. That was the beginning of a wonderful relationship between her and David.

Most people feel very helpless when a friend or relative has a child with Down syndrome. Do not hesitate to take up offers of help. Friends often need to do something constructive.

RESPONDING TO HURTFUL REMARKS

You will need to develop strategies for dealing with the occasional hurtful reaction, and it is worth while giving some thought to these early on, so that you do not find yourself unprepared.

- ### Set an example

People will often respond better to your example than your criticism. When someone uses an inappropriate term, do not point this out in an obvious way. Rather, repeat what they have said in a more appropriate way. For example, if someone says: 'A mongol lived near us who loved music', you could simply reply: 'Yes, many children with Down syndrome enjoy music.' Without confronting the person, he or she will hopefully realize that 'Down syndrome' is a preferable term to 'mongol'. Of course, if people do not take the hint, you may have to be more direct.

- ### Silent 'pep' talks

Some parents find that a good technique for helping them when they have just experienced a bad reaction from someone is to give themselves a silent 'pep' talk. This often cheers them up and makes them see the remark in perspective. It is also preferable to responding verbally in a way that may be regretted later. Parents tell me that they say things to themselves like 'keep going and this will soon be over' or 'this man obviously doesn't know what he is talking about.' You may find this technique helpful.

- **Rehearse responses**

  If you are going to experience a particularly difficult, but unavoidable situation, it may be worth while rehearsing the situation before it takes place. You can do this on your own or with someone close to you. You may want to rehearse the scene, looking at different ways it may develop. You will probably find that after this sort of role-playing, you will decide upon a series of responses that are more appropriate than those which would have occurred without rehearsal. Sometimes, these rehearsed responses can be used on subsequent occasions in similar situations.

- **Provide information**

  There are a number of pamphlets on Down syndrome published by Down syndrome associations in different parts of the world. Sometimes, it is easier to give one of these to a friend, rather than explaining the syndrome yourself.

3. What is Down syndrome?

There are more differences between children with Down syndrome than there are similarities. Your child will have many individual characteristics inherited from his parents. He may look like his mother, his father, a grandmother, or an aunt. His hair may be red, dark, or fair. His eyes may be blue, brown, green, or grey. He may be dark- or light-skinned. In fact, he could have any of the wide range of features that make us all look different from one another.

This is true not only of physical appearance, but also of temperament and range of abilities. Children with Down syndrome may be easy-going or strong-willed. Some like music, while others have no interest in it at all. Some are energetic, others less active. All have some degree of intellectual disability; but this may be mild in some and more marked in others. Ignore generalizations such as 'children with Down syndrome are placid and love music'; they are unlikely to be true of all children with the condition. Children and adults with Down syndrome vary enormously in appearance, temperament, and ability. Each one is a unique individual.

WHAT IS A SYNDROME?

Superimposed upon his individual characteristics, each child and adult with Down syndrome has features that he shares with others who have the syndrome. These common features are the hallmark of a syndrome.

A syndrome is a condition distinguished by a cluster of features occurring together. If a person has a number of the features associated with a particular syndrome, he is said to have that syndrome. A congenital syndrome, such as Down syndrome, is one which is present at birth. It is due to abnormal development of the fetus.

There are many thousands of different congenital syndromes, with new ones being reported every month. They are usually named after the first person who described them. In the case of Down syndrome, this was Dr J. L. Down.

HISTORICAL BACKGROUND

It is almost certain that there have always been people with Down syndrome. The earliest recorded representation of a person with the characteristic features of the condition dates back to an altar-piece in Aachen, Germany, painted in about 1505.

But Down syndrome does not seem to have been recognized as an entity until 1866, when Dr John Langdon Down (1828–1896), an English doctor working in Surrey, first described the characteristic features of the syndrome. Down did not understand the cause of the condition he had described. His suggestion that Down syndrome was a reversion to a primitive Mongolian ethnic stock, was soon repudiated by his son, Reginald, who was also a doctor.

Although de Waardenburg had suggested in 1932 that Down syndrome might be caused by a chromosomal abnormality,* it was some time before this was confirmed. In 1959, ninety-three years after Down's original description, Lejeune and his colleagues in Paris demonstrated that Down syndrome was associated with an extra chromosome.

TERMINOLOGY

People with Down syndrome were once referred to as having 'mongolism' or being 'mongols'. These terms arose because of the superficial resemblance between the appearance of people with the syndrome and that of oriental people. Such terms are out-of-date. We now use the terms 'Down syndrome' or 'Down's syndrome'. The former term is preferable, because Dr Down did not have the syndrome himself, nor did he 'own' it.

When describing your child's condition, you should say he has Down syndrome and not that he 'is a Down syndrome', as parents sometimes do. Describe him as 'a child with Down syndrome', rather than 'a Down syndrome child'. He is a child first and foremost. The fact that he has Down syndrome is of secondary importance.

---

* The nature of chromosomes, and the different types of Down syndrome, will be described in the next chapter.

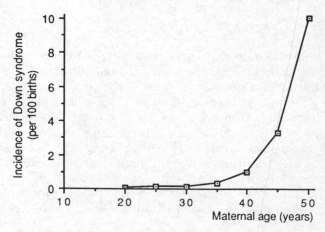

Fig. 3. Incidence of Down syndrome and maternal age.

HOW COMMON IS DOWN SYNDROME?

Down syndrome is one of the most common congenital syndromes. It is the most prevalent chromosomal disorder, and also the most frequently recognized cause of intellectual disability. It occurs approximately once in every seven hundred births, and is seen in all ethnic groups. There are slightly more boys born with Down syndrome than girls, but this difference is small. The reason for the slight predominance of males is unknown.

Maternal age

The chance of a woman having a child with Down syndrome increases with her age at the time of conception. The increase is particularly marked from about the age of 35 years (Fig. 3).

In most developed countries, pregnancies in women over the age of 35 years constitute less than 10 per cent of all pregnancies. It is for this reason that, despite an increased individual risk, women over 35 years give birth to only one-third of all children with the syndrome. It is, therefore, a misconception to think that children with Down syndrome are only born to older women. In fact, two-thirds of all children with the syndrome are born to mothers under 35 years, with 20 per cent of all children with the syndrome born to mothers who are under 25 years.

HOW DOWN SYNDROME IS RECOGNIZED

In most children with Down syndrome, the condition is recognized at or shortly after birth. In the majority of cases, the doctor will be quite certain of the diagnosis on the basis of the child's appearance alone. In some cases, he or she may suspect that the child has Down syndrome, but will need to await the result of a chromosome test before being certain. Very rarely, the features may not be very noticeable, and even an experienced doctor may not initially suspect that the child has the syndrome.

No child with Down syndrome has all the characteristic features

As many as 120 features have been described in Down syndrome. Many children with the syndrome have no more than six or seven of these. With the exception of some degree of intellectual disability, there is no feature of Down syndrome that is present in all individuals with the syndrome.

Anyone may have some of the features of the syndrome

Once the characteristic features of Down syndrome have been pointed out to parents, they often become concerned because they see some of these features in their other children or themselves. Any normal person may have one or two of the external features seen in Down syndrome. This is quite normal and is unconnected with the syndrome. It does not mean that the individual 'carries' the syndrome, or is affected by it in any way.

Characteristic features

In the past, great importance was attached to many minor features associated with the syndrome. This was because, prior to 1959, no test was available which could definitively establish whether a child had the syndrome or not. Many features were

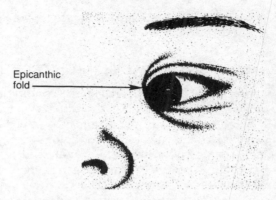

Fig. 4. Epicanthic fold.

therefore described and some characteristics, such as fingerprint patterns, were studied in great detail. This is no longer necessary.

The features listed below are those that are either particularly useful in recognizing the condition, or have some relevance to parents.

Face. When looked at from the front, the child with Down syndrome usually has a rounded face. From the side, the face tends to have a flat profile.
Head. The back of the head is slightly flattened in most people with Down syndrome. This is known as brachycephaly.
Eyes. The eyes of nearly all children and adults with Down syndrome slant slightly upwards. In addition, there is often a small fold of skin that runs vertically between the inner corner of the eye and the bridge of the nose (Fig. 4). This is known as the epicanthic fold or epicanthus. It is often seen in normal infants. In both normal children and those with Down syndrome it becomes less prominent, and may disappear, when the child grows older and the skin is taken up to cover the bridge of the nose. It is important only because prominent epicanthic folds may give a false impression of crossed eyes (squint) in children.

The eyes may have white or light-yellow speckling around the rim of the iris (coloured part of the eye). These specks are called Brushfield spots (Fig. 5), after an English doctor, Dr T.

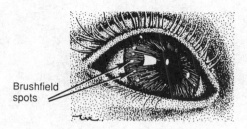

Brushfield
spots

Fig. 5. Brushfield spots.

Brushfield (1858–1937). These spots may also be present in the eyes of normal children. They often disappear later if the iris turns brown. Like epicanthic folds, they do not interfere with vision.

Hair. The hair of children with Down syndrome is usually soft and straight.

Neck. New-born babies with Down syndrome may have excess skin over the back of the neck, but this is usually taken up as they grow. Older children and adults tend to have short, broad necks.

Mouth. The mouth cavity is slightly smaller than average, and the tongue slightly larger. This combination encourages some children to acquire the habit of putting out their tongues at times. Parents can often stop this habit by teaching the child to keep his tongue in his mouth from early on, using techniques that will be described in Chapter 8.

Hands. The hands tend to be broad, with short fingers. The little finger sometimes has only one joint instead of the usual two. This finger may also be slightly curved towards the other fingers, a characteristic that runs in some families where it is unrelated to Down syndrome (Fig. 6). It is known as 'clino-dactyly.'

The palm may have only one crease going across it (Fig. 6) or, if there are two, both may extend right across the hand.

You may notice the doctor looking carefully at your child's fingerprints, which often have a characteristic pattern.

None of these hand variations causes any problem to the child, although the young child with Down syndrome may not be able to hold as much in his hand as other children.

Feet. These tend to be stubby, and to have a wide space ('sandal gap') between the first and second toes. This may be associ-

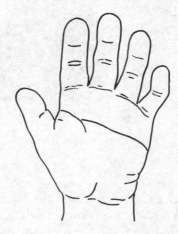

Fig. 6. Single palmar crease and incurved little finger.

ated with a short crease on the sole, which starts at this gap and runs back for a couple of centimetres.

Tone. The limbs and necks of young children with Down syndrome are often floppy. This muscular floppiness is called 'hypotonia', meaning 'low tone'. Tone is the resistance muscles give to being moved when they are relaxed. It is quite different from muscular strength, which requires active contraction of the muscle. The strength of the muscles is usually normal in children with Down syndrome. They may be floppy, but they are not usually weak.

Low tone is more marked in some children than others. Tone is always lowest during the early years, and improves spontaneously as the child gets older. This improvement is such that low tone is hardly ever a significant problem in adolescents or adults with the syndrome.

Body size. Children with Down syndrome usually weigh less than average at birth. Their length at birth is similarly reduced. During childhood, they grow steadily but slowly, and their ultimate height as adults is generally shorter than would be expected for their family. It is usually near the bottom of the normal range, and is approximately 145 to 168 cm in men and 132 to 155 cm in women.

4. How Down syndrome comes about

When parents are told that their new-born baby has Down syndrome, one of the first questions they ask is 'How did this happen?' Thanks to advances in the field of genetics, we can go a long way towards answering this question.

CELLS, CHROMOSOMES, AND GENES

To understand how Down syndrome comes about, we must first look at some of the smallest components of the body: the cells, the genes, and the chromosomes.

The human body is made up of tiny *cells* too small to be seen by the naked eye, but visible through a microscope. Each one of these cells is like a brick making up a building. All the cells of the body originate from one single cell formed by the fusion of the mother's egg and the father's sperm.

Each cell carries in its centre a small nucleus (Fig. 7), which can be thought of as a little bag filled with the genetic material (genes) that the individual has inherited from his or her parents.

There are approximately 100 000 *genes* in every nucleus. Each one controls the manufacture of one particular protein, and thereby determines one characteristic of the body. During adult life, we use only about 10 per cent of our genes at any one time. But during the development of the fetus in the womb nearly half the genes in each nucleus are being used simultaneously, to control the workings of the cells during this busy period of development. This means that genetic errors often result in abnormal development of the fetus.

The genes do not lie freely in the nucleus, but are grouped together like beads threaded on a string, in strands called *chromosomes*. Having the genes on the chromosomes is nature's way of keeping things tidy. When the cell divides to form two new cells, as the body grows, it allows orderly separation of the nucleus into two equal halves.

Each cell of the body has 46 chromosomes. The 46 consist of

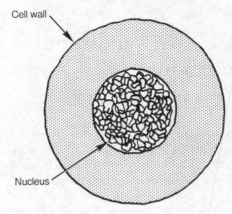

Fig. 7. Body cell.

23 pairs, each chromosome of a pair from one of the parents. Every time a cell divides into two, the new cells so formed consist of the same number of chromosomes, 46.

The only human cells which are different are the eggs and sperm, which have only half that number, that is, 23. This is necessary so that when an egg and a sperm fuse, a cell is formed consisting of the standard 46 chromosomes.

How chromosomes are seen

In order to look at chromosomes, body cells (usually from blood) are grown in the laboratory until there are many of them. The nuclei of these cells are broken open, and the chromosomes are stained in order to make them visible. They can then be seen through a microscope. Photographs can be taken through the microscope, and then the picture of each chromosome is cut out and mounted on a card in order of size (Fig. 9), starting with the largest.

Twenty-two of the chromosome pairs are given numbers in order to identify them. They are numbered according to size, starting with the largest as number one.

The pair without numbers are the sex chromosomes, which determine whether the fetus will develop into a male or a female. These chromosomes are represented by the letters 'X' and 'Y'. A male has an X and a Y: the X from the mother, the Y from the father. A female has two Xs: one from each parent.

THE CHROMOSOMAL ERROR IN DOWN SYNDROME

Down syndrome comes about when there is an extra number 21 chromosome. This additional chromosome, because of the genes it contains, causes an excessive amount of certain proteins to be formed in the cell. This disturbs normal growth in the body of the fetus. The particular proteins involved, and how they act, are not presently known.

As the fetus develops, the cells of the body do not divide as rapidly as they normally do, and this results in fewer body cells, and, therefore, a smaller baby. In addition, the migration of cells that occurs in the formation of different parts of the body is disrupted, notably in the brain. Once the individual with Down syndrome is born, all these differences are already present. The baby, having fewer brain cells and a different brain formation, will learn slowly. These changes are established before birth, and cannot be reversed afterwards.

The presence of an additional chromosome adversely affects fetal survival: 80 per cent of such pregnancies end in miscarriage. Children who are born with the syndrome may therefore be regarded as testimony to their mother's ability to support them during the pregnancy, despite this disadvantage.

It is now known that it is not necessary for a whole additional chromosome 21 to be present to cause Down syndrome. All that is needed is for an extra amount of a critical small portion of the chromosome to be present (see Fig. 8). The rest of chromosome 21, although usually also present in excess, does not appear to play any part in producing the syndrome.

DIFFERENT TYPES OF DOWN SYNDROME

All children with Down syndrome have the extra critical portion of chromosome 21 in their cells. But the amount of chromosome 21 present, and the way in which the error comes about, can take one of three forms.

It is important to distinguish between these different forms, as the chance of the parents' having another child with the

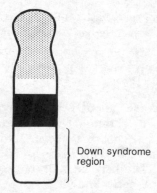

Down syndrome region

Fig. 8. Chromosome 21.

syndrome depends on which form their child has. In one of the forms, the degree to which the child shows the characteristics of the syndrome is also affected. The three forms are trisomy 21, translocation, and mosaicism. They are compared in Table 1.

1. Trisomy 21

The vast majority of children with Down syndrome (95 per cent), have an extra whole chromosome 21 in every cell of their body (Fig. 9). This is called trisomy 21 ('tri' = 'three' and 'somy' referring to the chromosome). This is the commonest form of Down syndrome in children born to mothers of any age. It results from one of the parents giving two number 21 chromosomes, rather than the usual one, to the child through the egg or the sperm.

Normally, when eggs or sperm are formed, a cell in the ovary or testicle divides to form two new cells, each with half the original number of chromosomes. It is from these cells that the eggs or the sperm originate. In the case of trisomy 21, this division is abnormal, and the egg or sperm receives an extra number 21 chromosome. This process is known as non-disjunction, because the pair of number 21 chromosomes in the original cell does not separate ('disjunct'), but remains together in one of the new cells.

We understand in general terms *how* non-disjunction occurs.

Table 1. Types of Down syndrome

Type	Incidence (%)	Chromosome findings	Physical features and intellectual disability
Trisomy 21	95	Extra chromosome 21 in every cell	Common form
Translocation	4	Extra part of chromosome 21 attached to another chromosome in every cell	Same as trisomy 21
Mosaicism	1	Mixture of cells, some with an extra chromosome 21, and others which are normal	Milder physical features and intellectual disability

During the process of the formation of an egg or sperm, the two number 21 chromosomes of the original cell come to lie together prior to cell division. Instead of each chromosome moving in an opposite direction to become part of one of the two new cells, they both move together. The new cells so formed consist of one cell with both number 21 chromosomes, and the other with no number 21 chromosome at all. The latter cannot survive, and soon disintegrates.

At present, we do not understand *why* non-disjunction occurs. It is unlikely to be caused by one factor alone. A number of factors must act together for non-disjunction to take place. Some factors that have been suggested, such as a genetic predisposition, exposure to radiation, and the presence of thyroid antibodies in the mother's blood, are probably unimportant. The most significant factor appears to be the mother's age. It should be emphasized that this is only one of many factors, most of which are presently unknown. Table 2 shows how the

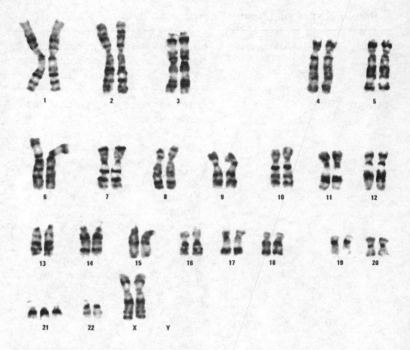

Fig. 9. Trisomy 21 in a female. There are three number 21 chromosomes instead of the usual two.

chance of having a child with Down syndrome increases with rising maternal age.

Non-disjunction does not always originate from the mother, as was once thought. In about 30 per cent of cases the extra chromosome comes from the sperm. This information is gained from special testing, where the parental origin of the extra chromosome can be determined. This is not done routinely, as it is technically a very difficult test to perform. But we now know that, when a child with this form of Down syndrome is born, it does not necessarily mean that the extra chromosome came from the mother.

While it is clear that maternal age is a significant factor in causing trisomy 21, the role of the father's age is less clear. There is conflicting evidence from studies in different parts of the world. Certainly, if the father's age does play a part, it is of so little significance that we do not need to take it into account.

Table 2. Incidence of Down syndrome and maternal age

Maternal age	Incidence of Down syndrome	Maternal age	Incidence of Down syndrome
20	1 in 2000	35	1 in 350
21	1 in 1700	36	1 in 300
22	1 in 1500	37	1 in 250
23	1 in 1400	38	1 in 200
24	1 in 1300	39	1 in 150
25	1 in 1200	40	1 in 100
26	1 in 1100	41	1 in 80
27	1 in 1050	42	1 in 70
28	1 in 1000	43	1 in 50
29	1 in 950	44	1 in 40
30	1 in 900	45	1 in 30
31	1 in 800	46	1 in 25
32	1 in 720	47	1 in 20
33	1 in 600	48	1 in 15
34	1 in 450	49	1 in 10

Parents often ask why the mother's age is important, while the father's age is not. When a female is born, all the eggs that her ovaries will produce during her lifetime are already present in an immature form. They then remain in a state of suspended animation until the particular cycle when that egg will be released. This means that they stay in that incomplete form for some twenty to forty years. It is not suprising that errors occur in a process which extends over such a long period of time. The older the woman, the longer the period of time, and, therefore, the greater the chance of this error.

In contrast to this, the formation of sperm does not begin until the male reaches puberty, and then there is a continuous ten-week cycle of sperm production. Sperm do not remain in one stage for very long, and are, therefore, less likely to have the particular error that results in trisomy 21.

2. Translocation

In about 4 per cent of cases, Down syndrome is due to the presence of an extra part, rather than the whole, of chromosome 21 (Fig. 10). This occurs when the small top portions of

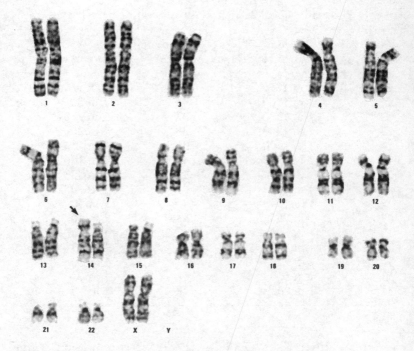

Fig. 10. Translocation 14/21 in a female. The arrow shows the composite chromosome consisting of part of chromosome 21 (top) and part of chromosome 14 (bottom).

chromosome 21 and another chromosome break off, and the two remaining portions stick to one another at their exposed ends. This process of one chromosome sticking on to another is called 'translocation' (Fig. 11). We still do not know why translocations occur, but we do know that, unlike what happens in the case of non-disjunction, parental age is not a factor.

Only certain chromosomes become involved in this sort of translocation with chromosome 21. They are chromosomes 13, 14, 15, or 22, or another chromosome 21 (14 is the most common). All of these chromosomes have small, genetically-inactive tips, which can break off and be lost without any ill effect.

Children with translocation Down syndrome do not differ from children with trisomy 21 Down syndrome in the degree

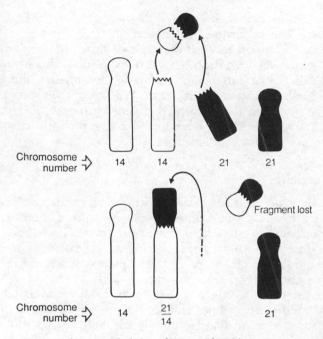

Chromosome number ⇗   14   14   21   21

Chromosome number ⇗   14   21/14   21

Fragment lost

Fig. 11. Origin of a translocation.

to which they are affected. The fact that children with translocation do not have the extra top part of the chromosome
makes no difference, because this is not a genetically important
part.

It is important for a chromosome test to be done on all
children with Down syndrome to detect those with a translocation, because, in about one-third of these children, one of the
parents will be found to be a carrier of Down syndrome. When
we say that someone 'carries' Down syndrome, we mean that,
while they themselves have no traces of the syndrome, they do
have a higher than usual chance of having a child with the
syndrome. A translocation carrier is normal, because he or she
has the usual 23 pairs of chromosomes. The only difference is
that one of his or her number 21 chromosomes is joined on to
one of the other chromosomes. This causes no problem to the
carrier personally; but when the time comes to produce an egg
or a sperm, it becomes more difficult to halve the number of

chromosomes evenly, because of the two which are joined. This will be discussed further in Chapter 16.

It should be remembered that, in two-thirds of cases where a child with Down syndrome has a translocation, this is not due to one of the parents being a carrier. In such cases, the translocation was an isolated error that occurred in the formation of the egg or sperm from which the child in question originated. Such a translocation is a random event, with little chance of recurrence in future pregnancies.

3. Mosaicism

In about 1 per cent of children with Down syndrome, there is an extra whole chromosome 21 in only a proportion of their body cells. The rest of their cells are normal. These individuals are said to exhibit mosaicism, because the cells of their body are like a mosaic made up of different pieces, some normal and some with the extra chromosome.

Mosaicism, as would be expected, is usually associated with less markedly affected individuals, because of the counteracting effect of the normal cells. Individuals with mosaicism often have less prominent physical features of Down syndrome, and develop and function closer to the normal range. Very rarely, individuals with this form of Down syndrome can be intellectually normal.

5. Your child's development

Your child with Down syndrome will develop and learn throughout his life. From a new-born baby, totally dependent on you for his every need, he will develop physically, intellectually, and emotionally, becoming more competent with every passing year. Children with Down syndrome always go forward in their development, but do so at a slower rate than other children.

For both normal children and those with Down syndrome, the eventual aim of childhood development is to gain independence. In all adults, independence is a relative term. We are all dependent on others to some degree. In Down syndrome, development is not only slower than normal, but is also less complete, and your child, in adulthood, will need more help than the average person.

RATE OF DEVELOPMENT

The normal child gains skills at an average rate. But the rate of development varies considerably from child to child. For example, some children get up and walk at nine months of age, while others, equally normal, will keep crawling until eighteen months.

Children with Down syndrome also vary in their rate of development, with some developing more slowly and others at a faster rate. Figure 12 shows graphically the difference between the development of normal children and children with the syndrome.

It is helpful, when thinking of the development of children, to use the analogy of cars travelling along a road. The normal child travels along the road of increasing skill-development at an average speed. The child with Down syndrome travels along the same road, picking up the same skills as he gets older. But because he travels along at a slower speed, he arrives at each stage of development at a later age than the normal child, and stays there for a longer period.

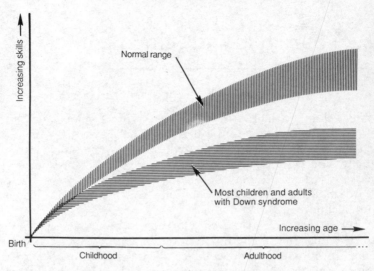

Fig. 12. Rate of development.

Figure 12 highlights two important aspects of development in the child with Down syndrome. The first is that the learning curve for children with Down syndrome does not stop increasing when adolescence ends. That is because it is a curve of skills, not a curve of intellectual processes. While it is true that in adulthood we use the same intellectual processes as in late adolescence, we are still able to learn new skills as we grow older. This sort of learning goes on in adults with Down syndrome as well. They do not stop learning in adulthood, as some parents have been led to believe. They too learn new things, provided that they are given appropriate opportunities. In fact, adulthood is often a time when people with Down syndrome are able to make great strides in learning new skills for living.

Secondly, Fig. 12 shows that, although the child with Down syndrome is travelling at a steady pace, the distance between him and the normal child increases as they get older. That is why you should not attach too much importance to the number of months or years your child is behind the normal child at any particular age. The important thing is that your child maintains a constant rate of development.

Maximum potential

Development is controlled by the brain. Children with Down syndrome have brains that are slightly differently formed from those of other children. This makes the process of learning new skills less efficient. We now know that, with appropriate education, children with Down syndrome can certainly develop more rapidly than was formerly thought possible; but they cannot 'catch up' with normal children. We should aim to help each child with Down syndrome develop to his own greatest potential. But one should not attempt to drive a child beyond his capacity. The result of placing such stress on children with Down syndrome is that they will usually perform less well, rather than better.

Stops and starts

Although the development of children with and without Down syndrome progresses at a steady rate when looked at over a period of months or years, development actually proceeds in a series of 'stops and starts'. The 'stops' are periods when children do not appear to be achieving new skills. These lulls in development are very necessary for children. During such phases they consolidate what they have already learned by practising their new skills. In addition, although it may not be apparent to the observer, they are beginning to develop components of future skills.

For example, a child with Down syndrome, aged seventeen months, who pulls himself from a crawling to a standing position while holding on to a low table, may frustrate his parents by not letting go and taking those first unsupported steps. If the parents watch him carefully, they will see that, although he seems 'stuck' in this stage of development, he is making progress. Firstly, by continually pulling himself up and moving sideways while holding on to the low table, he is improving his muscular power and his co-ordination in the upright position. Secondly, every time he side-steps around the table, he does so a little faster, a little more securely, and uses his arms a little less for support. He is like a gymnast practising the same series of movements again and again, until they become automatic and secure. Then, one day, when he is ready, and not before, he lets go and takes his first tottering steps.

46

The 'milestones' children reach in their development are just the observable 'tip of the iceberg'. Far more development goes on unseen beneath the surface. Once you realize that your child is developing, even when he does not seem to be, observing his development will become less frustrating for you.

AREAS OF DEVELOPMENT

Development is usually divided into different areas for the purpose of description. These areas are:

Gross-motor development

This is the development of skills that involve large groups of muscles. These skills include rolling, sitting, crawling, standing, walking, running, jumping, and hopping. Posture and movement of the body are involved. The term 'motor' refers to movement.

Fine-motor development

This refers to manipulation using the hands and fingers. Skills such as picking up objects, transferring them from hand to hand, using scissors, drawing, bead-threading, and block-building are all included. Co-ordination of the hands and eyes is involved, as well as a sense of space and direction, and the use of the two hands together.

Personal and social development

This is the area where development of self-help skills, as well as social skills, is involved. Self-help skills include finger-feeding, drinking from a cup, using the toilet, using eating utensils, washing, and dressing. Social skills involve appropriate reactions to people, such as distinguishing friends from strangers, and playing co-operatively with other children.

Language and speech development

Language refers to the grammatical structure and meaning of what is said. Speech relates to its clarity and fluency. Receptive language is the understanding of language, while expressive language is its use. Receptive language must always be in advance of expressive language, as words cannot be used appropriately until they are understood. Prior to language development, 'prelanguage' is already evident. This includes the different sorts of cries, 'turn-taking', and babbling, which are discussed later in this chapter. We should also not forget that a great deal of communication at any age is not in the form of words, but by gesture, facial expression, and posture.

Cognitive development

This refers to the application of abstract thought and reasoning to problem-solving, as well as the understanding of certain concepts, general knowledge, and many other abilities regarded as constituting that hard-to-define entity called 'intelligence'.

Overlap between different areas

Any attempt to divide development into different areas is artificial. There is a great deal of overlap between different areas. For example, drinking from a cup is a self-help skill as well as a fine-motor skill. Having a conversation is a language skill, but is also a social skill. Looking for an object hidden inside a box is a fine-motor skill, but also requires the cognitive skill of understanding that objects do not cease to exist when they are out of view. There are many such examples. Nevertheless, the concept of different areas of development is a useful one, provided we always remember that these areas are not totally separate entities.

REVIEW OF DEVELOPMENT

This review of development is based on the developmental progress of children who were living at home and had received some form of early intervention. In this review, I have described the development of an 'average child' with the syndrome. By this, I mean a child who is attaining all milestones at the average age for children with the syndrome. This is an artificial concept, as few, if any, children are average in every way. Most children with the syndrome will reach the milestones sooner or later than the exact age given. The ages given should, therefore, *only be regarded as a guide*.

Table 3 shows the average age and age-range when children with Down syndrome attain some of the major developmental milestones. The average ages and age-ranges for normal children are given for comparison. The age-ranges for children with the syndrome are very broad, because of a small number with associated conditions, such as severe heart disease or hearing impairment, which adversely affect their development.

Girls with the syndrome develop, on average, slightly faster than boys. This is true of normal girls as well; but in the case of Down syndrome, girls seem to have the edge on boys even as adults. The differences are small, however, and the review that follows is equally relevant to both sexes.

The new-born baby (the first four weeks of life)

During the new-born period, your baby is entirely dependent on you. His pleasures are being fed and feeling comfortable. This is the beginning of the bond that develops between you and your baby, a process that is not confined to this period, but will continue throughout infancy and early childhood.

Gross-motor development

The new-born baby with Down syndrome is usually floppier than a normal new-born. When you change his nappies, you may notice that he gives less resistance to separating the legs than a normal child. He may adopt a 'frog-legs' position when lying on his back. When he lies on his tummy, his legs may lie straight in line with his trunk, and his bottom may be flatter than that of a normal baby.

Fine-motor development

New-born babies, with and without Down syndrome, hold their hands clenched in a fist most of the time. They grasp tightly on anything that is placed in their hands (grasp reflex). This is not a voluntary action. They have poor control of their hands, and may scratch their faces in an attempt to move their hands towards their mouths.

Personal and social development

New-borns, both those with Down syndrome and those without, are far more alert and competent than was once thought.

Table 3. Major developmental milestones

	Down syndrome		Normal	
	Average age	Age range	Average age	Age range
Gross motor				
Sits alone	11 months	6–30 months	6 months	5–9 months
Crawls	15 months	8–22 months	9 months	6–12 months
Stands	20 months	$1-3\frac{1}{4}$ years	11 months	8–17 months
Walks alone	26 months	1–4 years	14 months	9–18 months
Language				
First word	23 months	1–4 years	12 months	8–23 months
Two-word phrases	3 years	$2-7\frac{1}{2}$ years	2 years	15–32 months
Personal/Social				
Responsive smile	3 months	$1\frac{1}{2}-5$ months	$1\frac{1}{2}$ months	1–3 months
Finger-feeds	18 months	10–24 months	10 months	7–14 months
Drinks from cup (unassisted)	23 months	12–32 months	13 months	9–17 months
Uses spoon	29 months	13–39 months	14 months	12–20 months
Bowel control	$3\frac{3}{4}$ years	2–7 years	22 months	16–42 months
Dresses self (not fastenings)	$7\frac{1}{4}$ years	$3\frac{1}{2}-8\frac{1}{4}$ years	4 years	$3\frac{1}{4}-5$ years

Every new-born is different, and while some new-born babies with Down syndrome are sleepy individuals who may have to be woken up for feeds, others are very alert, and spend a lot of time awake. Some may be irritable, and cry for no apparent reason.

The baby with Down syndrome usually has a soft cry, because of the low tone of the muscles between the ribs and over the abdomen. These muscles are used to push air out of the chest during crying. For the same reason, his sucking may be less effective, and feeding may take a little longer. With patience and perseverance, most babies with Down syndrome can be successfully breast-fed.

Language development

New-born babies with Down syndrome usually seem to be very responsive to the sounds they hear. They jerk their arms and bring up their legs in response to loud sounds (Moro reflex). This is a normal reaction for a new-born.

Young babies, both those with and without Down syndrome, exhibit a behaviour in response to language that is called 'turn taking'. This is best observed when the child is in a relaxed state. The parent starts talking to the baby, and, in response, the baby stops his usual random movements. Instead, he makes smaller movements of the limbs, following the rhythm of the parent's voice. When the parent stops talking, the baby responds by making noises or moving his lips, while increasing the movements of his limbs. If the parent stops responding and gives the baby a blank look, the infant appears puzzled, and may move in an exaggerated way, as if to gain the parent's attention. Some babies even look dejected, and may remain in this state for a few seconds. When talking to your baby, it is, therefore, important to pause occasionally, in order to give him a chance to 'take his turn'.

- ### Things to do with your new-born baby

The new-born period is a difficult one for parents of a child with Down syndrome because they are still coming to terms with the diagnosis. New-born babies are demanding, because of the frequent feeds and changing of nappies. It is not important for you to attempt to 'stimulate' your new-born child with Down syndrome. At this stage, all that is important is to satisfy his needs for food, warmth, and comfort. He will benefit from your closeness, being cuddled, and having you talk to him. What he will most enjoy looking at is your face, and this is far more important than any toy or mobile you may place around him.

The first year (from one month to one year)

During the course of the first year, the average infant with Down syndrome makes rapid strides in all areas of development. This is usually most apparent during the second half of the year. Perhaps the most dramatic change is in the child's responsiveness. During the year, he changes from a sleepy little infant into a socially responsive and charming one-year-old.

Gross-motor development

During the first six months, low tone often makes gross-motor development lag behind other areas. After this period, gross-motor development tends to keep pace with other areas of development, although tone may still remain fairly low.

By the end of the first year, the average infant with Down syndrome is able to sit on his own without any support. When placed on his tummy at this time, he tries very actively to crawl, but does not make any progress.

Fine-motor development

Towards the middle of the first year, the average child with Down syndrome begins to reach for objects out of his grasp. As the year progresses, he learns to play with them. At this stage, 'play' consists of putting the object in his mouth, or shaking or banging it. This is a very important phase, when control of the hands increases, and the infant learns to manipulate objects and discover what their possibilities are.

By the end of the year, he is able to hold objects in both hands (if they are placed there), transfer an object from hand to hand, and pick up small objects using his fingers and palm to 'rake' them up.

By the end of the first year, his concept of objects has developed; and if something falls out of sight, he looks for it, rather than treating it as if it has vanished, as he did formerly.

Personal and social development

The first year is a time of marked increase in the responsiveness of the average child with Down syndrome.

At about two or three months of age, while looking at an adult, his face breaks out into a happy smile—a wonderful moment for parents. From three months, he begins to recognize familiar faces, although it is not until about twelve months that he is likely to show displeasure at being handed to a stranger. This response varies from child to child, and to some degree, depends on how many different people the child usually comes into contact with during infancy.

By the end of the year, he is clearly more assertive and vigorous, and resists having a toy taken from him. By this age he is also able to drink from a cup, provided that it is held for him.

Language development

The young child communicates by different cries, each indicating different needs. At the beginning of the first year, parents usually start recognizing their child's distinctive cry as different from that of other children. They also notice that they can tell from the cry whether their child is hungry, uncomfortable, or tired.

Babbling increases over the first year, and by six months the average child with the syndrome enjoys very noisy babbling (razzing). This is a form of preparation for later speech.

Cognitive development

It will be clear from the age of six months that the average child with Down syndrome is beginning to reason and remember in a more obvious way. The child's understanding that objects do not cease to exist when out of view, and his recognition of familiar faces, are evidence of this.

- **Things to do with your infant during the first year**

You still remain the most important 'object' in your child's world. The consistency of your attention and your interaction with your child will help him develop more than anything else you do.

Do not forget to talk to him. Talk to him about the things you are doing and about the objects around you. If he makes sounds, respond. Look at him and talk back to him as though you were having a conversation. Do not worry about sounding silly. Talking to a young baby will soon become natural. Research has shown that many nine-month-old children with Down syndrome prefer nursery rhymes recited correctly, to the same rhymes with the words recited in reverse, but with the correct rhythm and intonation. This indicates a recognition of words as such, even if their meaning is not yet understood.

In the first few months, when he is becoming better at looking at and following objects, he may enjoy colourful toys hung about his cot, particularly if they make a soft noise which draws his attention to them. It is important to realize that infants respond best to soft noises at this stage. The tinkling of bells or soft chimes is the most appropriate. When he begins to reach for and hold objects, you need to make certain that the toys he is given are bright, easy to hold, and safe when put into his mouth. They should be of a variety of colours, shapes, and textures. Initially toys can be suspended from a frame in front of him. Later, when he is sitting unsupported, they can be placed around him, and he will be able to choose what he wants.

The second year of infancy (age one to age two)

During the second year, the average child with Down syndrome is preoccupied with his developing mobility. Development in other areas progresses slowly in the mobile infant. Greater competence in manipulation and language emerges tentatively, although he often reverts to the more immature fine-motor and verbal experimentations of the first year.

Gross-motor development

During the second year of life, the average child with Down syndrome progresses from sitting on his own, through crawling, to eventual standing. Most children do not walk unaided until the beginning of the following year.

Crawling is not a particulary important milestone, and is often over-emphasized. Children with Down syndrome, like normal children, sometimes do not go through a crawling stage. This is not important, as some of the earliest walkers are those who do not crawl.

Getting around before walking can take a variety of forms. Low tone in the lower limbs makes many children with Down syndrome drag their legs behind them as they pull themselves along with their arms ('commando' crawling). Some children shuffle about on their bottoms, or roll from side to side in order to get from one place to another.

Eventually, the day arrives when, after many failed attempts, the child pulls himself up to a standing position in his cot, or using a low table or chair. Once in this upright position, and very pleased with himself, he starts side-stepping while holding on to furniture to grasp objects that are out of reach (cruising). To get from one place to another, where no supporting surface exists, he goes down on all fours and crawls. After a time, he lets go and takes the first few tottering steps, only to fall down again. With time, more and more steps are taken. Until this stage is reached, the child often enjoys walking with some support, such as a small cart.

Fine-motor development

By the beginning of the second year the average child with Down syndrome is becoming more adept at picking up small objects, and is now able to point with his index finger. He is also able to use this finger together with the thumb to pick up a small object, such as a raisin, in a 'pincer grasp'.

At this stage, having learned how to hold on to an object, the child learns a new skill—how to let go. One day, it occurs to him that if he lets go of an object, while at the same time making a sweeping motion of his wrist, the object flies away. It often happens that children with Down syndrome get 'stuck' on this behaviour for a variable period of time at this stage. Such a child often throws, or 'casts', as it is called, everything that gets into his hands. This can be an extremely frustrating time for parents, especially those impatient for their child to learn more constructive skills such as block-building, puzzles, and drawing. All children go through this stage, but in some children with Down syndrome, it seems to be particularly accentuated and prolonged. If this occurs it is best for parents to hide their feelings of frustration and not make a fuss, or the child will only persist with this behaviour. Parents should not replace everything immediately, as this gives the child an incentive to throw it again. Plans to encourage the child to do form-boards and other fine-motor activities should be deferred until this stage has passed. Children always outgrow this behaviour. Even those who do not throw things may show very little interest in fine-motor tasks at this stage.

Personal and social development

Under the age of one, most children with Down syndrome are quite content in the arms of a stranger. But after their first birthday, they often undergo a temporary change. This is as a result of the normal development of the ability to distinguish strangers from people with whom the child is familiar. In some children, the negative response to strangers is initially exaggerated, and the child may start crying whenever he sees a new face, or cling to his parents when out. It is best to be patient with the child at this stage, as this behaviour will invariably settle down.

If your child is very frightened of strangers, hold him when entering a place where there are new faces. Keep him with you until he feels comfortable enough to make the first move. Try to dissuade well-meaning strangers from making advances to him until he has become used to them. Once he feels confident, he may make short forays, but will usually return to your side when he feels insecure. With time, he will feel more at ease, and will begin to make friendly overtures to strangers spontaneously.

By the end of the second year, the average child with Down syndrome manages a half-full cup on his own and is able to finger-feed. He is also able to wave 'bye-bye', and enjoys interactive games such as 'clap-handies'.

Language development

During the second year, the average child with the syndrome shows an increased understanding of language. An understanding of the purpose of familiar objects is shown by the 'definition-by-use' play, in which the child, when given an object, plays with it in an appropriate way (a spoon is put in the mouth, a brush on the head), thus demonstrating the presence of an 'inner language'.

He begins carrying out simple requests such as 'ta', or 'give me', by giving an object he is holding. At this stage, he 'talks' a lot in his own jargon (nonsense language), and this can be heard particularly when he is alone in his cot.

The age at which children with Down syndrome say their first word, as in the case of normal children, is one of the most variable of all the milestones of development. The average child with Down syndrome is saying one or two words by his second birthday. A 'word' is any group of sounds that the child uses consistently and appropriately. Initially words are over-generalized, for example, every animal is called a 'doh' ('dog'). Specific words for each kind of animal come later. The child always understands more than he can say, and he may point to certain parts of his body on request, even though he cannot yet name them.

When learning new words, children engage in what is called 'referential looking'. The child looks at an object, and the parent follows his line of vision to see what has caught the child's attention. The parent then names what they are both looking at, and in this way, the child learns the name of the object.

Cognitive development

The average child with Down syndrome shows a more sophist-icated concept of objects by the end of the second year. His understanding of shape means that he is able to place a circular inset in a round hole. He still resorts to banging objects and putting them into his mouth from time to time. His greater understanding that objects continue to exist even when they cannot be seen means that he looks for a hidden object, such as a wrapped sweet, with more persistence. Towards the end of the year, he understands that objects can be used as 'tools', and the link between an action and its consequence becomes clearer. He will, for example, tug at a table-cloth to obtain an object out of reach.

● **Things to do with your infant during the second year**

At this age, your child will probably enjoy playing interactive games with you, such as 'clap handies' and 'pat-a-cake'. He may enjoy 'peek-a-boo', and be keen to wave 'bye bye' when leaving friends.

When crawling about, your child will enjoy open spaces, and it is best to move furniture away, as children easily get trapped underneath. A rolling ball may provide fun and incentive to the crawling baby, who pushes it a little way and then crawls after it.

A low coffee table, without sharp edges, is useful when a child is at the cruising stage. He may enjoy having a number of toys on it, which, once grasped, are usually thrown to the floor.

This is the age when attention should be given to child-proofing your house. Dangerous objects and substances should be out of reach. Unnecessary stress may be prevented by putting all fragile ornaments beyond his reach.

Once your child is walking with support, a cart to push around is fun; but it must be well-balanced. A brick in the cart will give it more stability. Baby-walkers are also a great help at this stage, and, unlike certain children with increased tone, children with Down syndrome will not be harmed by walking in these.

Perhaps the game which children enjoy most once they have moved out of the throwing phase, is putting objects into containers and then taking them out again. You can provide cooking pots or small boxes as containers. Any object large enough not to be swallowed, but small enough to fit in the hand, is suitable. Children will often enjoy this activity for long periods at this age.

Referential looking helps your infant understand communication, as well as learn the names of objects. In addition to objects, you should show him simple pictures in books and tell him a little about them.

Parents often ask how they can stimulate their child's language. It is by responding to your child's attempts to speak that you help him best. When he names something, expand the words he says into a sentence, or comment on what he has said. Do not correct his speech. It is best to repeat what he has said correctly, but not to comment any further. In this way, he will eventually copy what you say.

The toddler (age two to age three)

With walking, the toddler takes a major step towards greater independence. Teaching him to accomplish things for himself, while accepting the demands of others, is a special challenge at this age.

Gross-motor development

Between the ages of two and three, the average child with Down syndrome becomes more adept at gross-motor tasks. By the end of the third year, he walks with such control that he can pull a small toy along on a string and walk up stairs if his hand is held. By the age of three, he has developed such good co-ordination that he can seat himself on a small chair. He is also able to kick a small ball.

With this development in gross-motor ability, the child is active and curious, but has very little notion of common dangers. He needs to be closely supervised.

Fine-motor development

At this age, the average child with Down syndrome is easily distracted, and cannot concentrate on a task for long. This is not a sign of 'hyperactivity' as a specific disorder, but rather an indication of the child's developmental immaturity. As with all children, it improves as he gets older.

Throwing objects has stopped by now, and he is also less likely to put them in his mouth, or bang or shake them. Simple form-boards can now be completed, and, by the end of the second year, he is able to do a large two-piece inset, even if it is turned around to confuse him. He is able to stack toys early in the year, and build towers of a few blocks by the end of the year. Towards the end of the third year, he can pour liquids from one cup to another without spilling.

Getting the child to do all these things is made easier by a tendency to imitate at this age. This shows itself in his attempts to copy things his parents do around the house (domestic mimicry), usually with an accuracy that shows close observation.

Personal and social development

Increased capability brings with it an increased desire for autonomy and more wilfulness at this age. The easy one-to-two-year-old becomes more difficult. He uses the 'automatic negative', saying 'no' to everything without giving it any consideration. Nearly all children go through these 'terrible two's', and parents should not become concerned that this indicates a difficult temperament. This is a stage a child must go through in order to increase his self-sufficiency; he will become more reasonable with time. Temper tantrums may be frequent, and he often insists on doing things for himself. Mood swings are common, and he may display a tantrum at one moment and be delightful the next. His changes of mood are probably as confusing to him as they are to his parents.

Children with Down syndrome often have difficulty chewing, and will display a preference for softer food. By the middle of the third year, they usually start coping with slightly tougher food; but many children with the syndrome may not want to chew meat or other fibrous food until five or six years of age.

From thirty months onward, toilet training is usually possible. One should wait until it is clear that the child can anticipate when he is about to pass urine or pass a motion.

The first step is to get your child used to the potty, by giving him a chance to sit on it fully clothed. If at this stage, or any later stage, your child reacts negatively to toilet training, you should avoid any fuss and defer training for a couple of weeks or months until he is ready. You should introduce your child to the idea of passing a motion in the potty by explaining that 'this is what big children do'. It may be helpful to give him an opportunity to see other children using a potty. There are a number of books which introduce children to the idea of using the potty* or the toilet†.

Put your child on the potty for short periods (say two to five minutes) at the time that you know he usually passes a motion. If there is no clear pattern, put him on the potty three times a day (after each meal). Eventually your patience will be rewarded, and the child will pass a motion, in which case you should give him plenty of praise. You will still need to remind him to use the potty for some time, and you should expect the occasional accident for the next year or so.

Language development

In the average child with the syndrome, language develops rapidly during the third year. The child has far greater language comprehension, and is able to fetch familiar objects on request. By the end of the third year, he is able to put two words together in a sentence. Sentences are still very simple, but represent a great increase in his ability to express himself. The first sentences usually consist of a noun (the agent) and an action word. The action word may be a conventional verb such

* 'Once upon a potty', Frankel, A. (Barron).
† 'All by myself', Gillham, B. (Methuen).

as 'go' ('Daddy go'), or a 'pivot' word used as a verb ('Daddy bye-bye'—meaning 'Daddy go').

In a number of children with Down syndrome, language development lags behind other areas. Children who are having particular difficulty acquiring language are often helped by learning to 'sign and say'. A speech therapist may teach such a child to use hand signs in addition to attempting words. Although the word may not be comprehensible, the sign often is. Parents sometimes worry that their child will continue to sign instead of speaking, but this is not the case. The use of signs reduces the child's frustration, improves his communication skills, and facilitates his acquisition of language. Many children who are taught signs will develop clearer speech, and, eventually, stop using the signs. The signs taught usually follow the 'Makaton' system, using one simple sign for each word. The particular signs used vary from country to country. The first signs taught are for those words which the child needs most in everyday communication, such as 'biscuit', 'drink', and 'toilet'.

• Things to do with your toddler

The toddler with Down syndrome usually enjoys water play; pouring with containers in the bath or paddling pool. He will probably enjoy feeling different textures, and play-dough and finger-painting are popular at this stage. Picture books become more important, and he may enjoy hearing an adult tell him a simple 'story' about the pictures. He will usually copy what his parents do about the house, and it is useful if pots, pans, old telephones, etc., are made available for play. Large toy versions are adequate, but usually not as popular as the real thing.

Toys that respond to manipulation are good at this age. A toy that pops open or rings a bell when something is pushed or turned is usually far more interesting than puzzles or blocks. Hands are still not strong, so any buttons or levers must be easy to manipulate.

With increased mobility, the child may now enjoy going on walks. He cannot be expected to stay at an adult's side, and will need to be followed closely.

The pre-schooler (age three to age five)

The average child with Down syndrome now begins to enjoy the company of other children. He needs to learn sharing, and this is something he learns from other children as much as from his parents. In fact, much of his learning at this age comes from copying his peers.

Gross-motor development

The pre-schooler becomes competent in this area of development. By the age of three years, the average child with Down syndrome manages stairs alone. Initially, stairs are taken two feet per step, but by five years he is alternating feet, one on each step, when going upstairs. He does not alternate going downstairs until seven or eight years of age.

At three and a half years, he is able to bring a small chair to a table and seat himself. At four and a half years, his leg control is so well developed that he copies movements such as crossing and uncrossing his legs and feet, and walks a short distance on tip-toe. He now throws and kicks a ball with greater accuracy. His running becomes better co-ordinated by five years, and he is able to change course to avoid objects in his path. At this age he can pedal a tricycle.

Fine-motor development

By three, the average child with the syndrome is able to open a small jar with a turning motion. He can also draw a perpendicular line in imitation, and by the end of the third year, can copy a horizontal line. By three years, he is able to turn pages, one at a time. By the age of four years, with some practice, he threads beads. He is now more willing to pack toys away, and even packs small objects into a box. He is also more adept at puzzles, and is able to build high towers with several blocks. By five years of age, he can copy a circle.

Personal and social development

At three to four years, the average child with Down syndrome has settled down considerably, and, although negative at times, is easier to control and more self-sufficient. Toilet training is well under way. Reliability in this regard takes time, and it is only towards five years of age that he pulls his pants up and down, and washes his hands after using the toilet.

At four years, he eats more independently at the table, only needing assistance with cutting up food. He is better able to tolerate other children around him, but still plays his own game near to other children, rather than with them.

Most three- to four-year-old children with Down syndrome

will separate from their parents without too much trouble, which means that attendance at a pre-school centre or class is now possible.

Language development

The average pre-schooler with the syndrome gives his first name on request, and names many objects. His sentences increase in length, and new parts of speech, such as pronouns, and later adjectives and adverbs, are introduced. He still makes errors in grammar, and words are often mispronounced. Words are left out of sentences, and the wrong word may be used. One sound is often substituted for another, and certain sounds are omitted from words. He is now able to listen to more complex stories and nursery rhymes, and can often repeat these. Communication still remains more of a monologue than a two-way conversation. He asks questions of the 'what' variety ('what is that?'), but is not yet asking the 'where', 'who', and 'why' questions. These usually occur at about six to ten years.

Cognitive development

At this age, intellectual function usually becomes easier to assess. Memory improves, and the average child with the syndrome is able to repeat short number-sequences he has just heard. He is beginning to understand concepts of size, and knows the difference between large and small. He is better able to solve problems mentally, and does not rely totally on actual experimentation to achieve solutions. This can be seen in the way puzzles are attempted, with pieces being manipulated into the correct spatial configuration before placement.

• Things to do with your pre-schooler

This is often a period when children attend pre-school groups or classes, and are learning a great deal from their peers. At home you will still need to give some thought to organizing your child's play. Children at this age usually need to be given some initial direction in their play, or they become bored and restless.

During the pre-school years, most children enjoy pretending to be adults (Fig. 13). As they grow older, their fantasy games become more elaborate, and their props smaller and more symbolic.

Fig. 13. Robbie, aged three and a half.

Drawing and painting are popular at this age. Pasting is also fun, although he will probably not be able to use a pair of scissors until about six years of age.

Primary-school years (age five to twelve)

This section covers the period from about five years until the onset of puberty. Adolescence will be discussed in a separate chapter.

The primary-school years are a time when the average child with Down syndrome develops a growing sense of his own competence. The ability to perform school-related tasks leads to increased self-esteem, which, in turn, influences his ability to develop social relationships.

Gross-motor development

Gross-motor skills become more refined during this time. Tone in the muscles increases, and joints lose some of their abnormal mobility. By ten years he can climb, swing, and slide, and is able to catch balls fairly well. From then onwards strength, co-ordination, and endurance show steady improvement.

Fine-motor development

By the age of ten years, the average child with the syndrome is able to draw a recognizable human figure, and simple representations of a house and other familiar objects are made. Folding, cutting, threading, and pasting are also becoming more accurate and rapid at this age. Between the ages of ten and twelve more and more shapes can be copied, and a few letters of the alphabet and numbers can be recognized and reproduced.

Personal and social development

Children with Down syndrome are usually better at everyday activities in the self-help and social spheres than may be anticipated from their intellectual ability.

The average child with Down syndrome can use a knife for cutting from about ten years. Dressing is more independent, although it may be slow. Buttons are mastered by ten years. Bathing independently, using a toothbrush, blowing the nose, and combing and brushing hair are also mastered at about this age.

Language development

As the child goes through school, his speech becomes clearer and his sentences longer. By twelve years, the average child with the syndrome has a vocabulary of about 2000 words. Despite this, he may be shy, and not talk much when out. At home, he is often more talkative, asking many questions. At about six to seven years, 'where' and 'who' questions are asked; and at about ten years, the 'why' variety follows. Language, however, is the most variable area of development in children with Down syndrome, and, in many, lags behind other areas.

Cognitive development

Throughout this period, the average child with the syndrome remains very concrete in his thinking, and understands things in a literal sense. He believes that causes are motivational: for example, the reason an apple falls from a tree is 'because it wants to'. He understands everything around him in the light of an internal model of the world, without modifying this on the basis of his experience (for example, 'storks bring babies', 'Father Christmas visits every house'). Rules are seen as rigid, and he may become confused by flexibility or exceptions.

- **Things to do with your school-aged child**

School, and school-related activities, will now take up much of your child's time. When children with Down syndrome first start school, they often have a poor sense of time-sequence. It may be helpful if you discuss the day's programme with your child at the beginning of each day. A wall-chart, with the programme for each day pictorially represented, is often helpful. Your child will probably find the chart easiest to understand if there is a separate sheet of paper for each day of the week, and only one day is put up at a time.

Activities such as cooking, shopping, and gardening are excellent opportunities for fun as well as for learning. Tasks must be within the child's capabilities, and praise should be given for effort rather than for accomplishment alone. You will need to give your child opportunities to do things for himself, even if it takes longer than it would if you did the task for him. This allows him to get better by practice, and improves his self-esteem. You can make things easier by ensuring that there is enough time to dress, making certain that clothes are easy to fasten, and ignoring slight untidiness. Try to break up tasks into small steps, and teach one step at a time, with rewards for success.

Try to answer your child's questions simply. Remember that he understands things in a very concrete way, and may not yet be able to think in a logical, abstract manner. When he makes errors in language or speech, do not comment on them. If he makes an incorrectly worded statement, or mispronounces a word, repeat what he has said in the correct way, and expand his comment. If he asks a question, answer using the correct words. Let your child tell you his experiences. Read books to him, and encourage him to tell you the stories too. Regular visits to the library will encourage an interest in books.

You need to provide opportunities for your child to spend time with friends after school. He still needs you to take some part in structuring his play. Crafts, hobbies, and games should be encouraged provided they are within his capabilities. Some recreational options that may help your school-aged child are described in Chapter 9.

6. Your child's health

The child with Down syndrome can now look forward to a longer, healthier life than ever before. This change in the general health of children and adults with Down syndrome is due to improved detection and treatment of those conditions which were responsible for much ill health and suffering in the past.

The majority of children with Down syndrome will be born without a heart defect, and will be active and vigorous children who suffer little ill health. The notion that all children with Down syndrome are frail, and liable to have repeated infections throughout their lives, is certainly false.

HOW TO READ THIS CHAPTER

This chapter contains two sections. The first deals with health maintenance, and should be read by all parents. The second section deals with conditions that are more common in children with Down syndrome. This section will only apply to parents of children who develop one of these conditions. It is meant as a reference, to be consulted if needed.

SECTION 1: KEEPING HEALTHY

Like all children, children with Down syndrome benefit from a healthy lifestyle. This includes living in a caring home environment, eating a balanced diet, and having adequate fresh air and exercise. Children with Down syndrome should not be overprotected. They benefit from the opportunity to lead active lives with varied experiences.

In addition to a healthy lifestyle, you will need to ensure that your child has regular checks to detect health problems early, before they have a chance to do widespread damage and become difficult to treat. This means that every child with Down syndrome should follow a systematic schedule of examinations and tests during her life. This may seem to be a bother; but the checks are well worth the trouble, to prevent the far greater

Fig. 14. Brad, aged 12, having just completed his fifth 'City to Surf' run. This is an annual event covering a 14-kilometre course through Sydney.

inconvenience that may arise from not detecting problems early. The routine checks are discussed below, and are summarized in Table 4.

- **New-born examination**

  The first health check is the examination of the new-born baby shortly after birth. This should be performed by a paediatrician, and should take place in front of the parents, so that they have a chance to see what is done and ask questions.

  As part of the new-born's examination, the doctor will examine the heart and blood vessels very carefully, to detect any

Table 4. Routine health checks

Examination/Test	Frequency
Physical examination	At birth and age six weeks, then annually
Thyroid blood test	At birth, six months, one year, then annually
Vision test	Annually from age 9–12 months until 10 years, then every two years
Hearing test	Annually from age 9–12 months until 10 years, then every two years
Dental check	Annually from age 2 years
Neck X-ray*	At 3–4 years and at 10 years

* Only if engaging in certain activities (see text)

signs that the child has been born with a heart abnormality. But as the heart is still undergoing a dramatic change after the baby has moved from the non-breathing state in the womb to become a breathing new-born, some heart disorders cannot be detected until a later check is done, when the child is about six weeks old. To rule out heart disease, some doctors will arrange non-traumatic tests of the heart, such as an electrocardiograph and echocardiogram (ultra-sound scan of the heart), at the six-week check. At this time, the paediatrician will also be able to monitor how growth has progressed, and gain more information about vision and hearing.

The only special blood tests which need to be done during the new-born period are the chromosome and thyroid tests. The chromosome test should be performed on the blood of all children with Down syndrome, even if the diagnosis seems certain from the baby's external appearance. In the case of translocation, both parents should also have a chromosome test. The chromosome test is discussed in more detail in Chapter 4.

The other test performed in the new-born period is a test of thyroid function. This blood test is usually done routinely on all new-born children to detect early thyroid deficiency, so that it can be treated before causing intellectual deterioration. Thyroid disorder in Down syndrome is discussed later in this chapter.

- **Vision tests**

  The first detailed test of vision should be done between nine months and a year by an eye specialist (ophthalmologist). After the age of one year, a child with Down syndrome should have annual checks of her vision by an ophthalmologist until ten years of age. Thereafter, checks should be performed every second year.

- **Hearing tests**

  Routine hearing tests are important in people with Down syndrome because they are susceptible to a condition known as 'glue ear', which can result in hearing loss. Glue ear is described later in this chapter.

  Hearing should first be tested between nine and twelve months. Thereafter, hearing should be checked on an annual basis until the age of ten. After ten years of age, it should be checked every second year.

  It is important to realize that hearing tests should be performed even if the child or adult seems to hear well. Mild hearing loss, affecting only certain sound frequencies, may go undetected unless proper hearing tests are performed. Such hearing loss can interfere with language comprehension, speech acquisition, and learning ability.

- **Neck X-ray**

  A neck X-ray should be performed on all children who will engage in activities which put the neck under strain, such as: tumbling, forward rolls, trampolining, diving, butterfly-stroke in swimming, high jump, break-dancing, contact sports, and rough-housing. This is done to exclude instability of the first two neck bones, a condition know as atlanto-axial instability. This condition is discussed in some detail later in this chapter.

  The first X-ray should be performed at about three to four years of age, or earlier if the child is about to start any of these activities. Even if the X-ray is normal, a repeat X-ray should be performed at around ten years of age.

- **Physical examinations**

  Every child with Down syndrome should be examined by a doctor once a year. This can be done by your child's paediatrician or at the annual visit to a child development clinic. The examination allows monitoring of growth, as well as detection of any new health problems. Annual medical examinations should continue throughout adulthood as well.

- **Blood tests**

  The only routine blood test that needs to be done is the measurement of the level of thyroid hormone. This will allow detection of low levels, which occur more commonly in individuals with Down syndrome of all ages. The test is important because early thyroid hormone deficiency is almost impossible to detect in any other way. Blood collection from infants and younger children should be performed by someone experienced in this procedure. Ask your paediatrician or the doctor at the child development clinic to arrange this for you. The level should be checked at birth, at six months, at one year, and then annually. Thyroid hormone disorders in Down syndrome are discussed later in this chapter.

- **Dental checks**

  A child with Down syndrome should visit a dentist for the first time at two years of age. Thereafter, the teeth should be checked every year. At these visits, in addition to examining the teeth, advice will be given on how to use dental floss and brush the teeth. The dentist will also have an opportunity to clean the teeth properly at these visits. Dental checks are particularly important in children who have heart abnormalities, because in these children a tooth infection can cause bacteria to grow in the heart (see next chapter).

Immunizations

It is important that children with Down syndrome are immunized. They should follow the usual immunization schedule, and can be given the whooping-cough immunization unless they have a specific problem such as seizures, or a history of severe reaction (not just redness at the site of the injection) to a previous whooping-cough immunization. Parents should avoid postponing immunizations because of a runny nose or a slight cough. Immunizations can be given during such minor illnesses without concern.

SECTION 2: CONDITIONS THAT ARE MORE COMMON IN CHILDREN WITH DOWN SYNDROME

When a child with Down syndrome has an illness, parents usually want to know if it has anything to do with the syndrome. Most children with Down syndrome enjoy good health. When they do become ill, they usually suffer normal childhood illnesses unrelated to the syndrome. These do not usually have to be treated differently because the child has Down syndrome.

Nevertheless, there are some conditions that are more common in children with the syndrome. Reading about these can cause unnecessary alarm if you do not keep things in perspective. Firstly, the conditions that are more common in Down syndrome are usually very mild or easily treated, such as constipation, upper respiratory tract infections, and dry skin. The more severe conditions also described below are much rarer. Most occur in only about one in a hundred children with the syndrome. This means that for every one child affected, ninety-nine children will not have the condition.

Upper respiratory tract infections

Infections of the upper respiratory tract (ears, nose, and throat) are not as troublesome to children with Down syndrome as is often claimed. But there are some children with the syndrome who seem to get more than their fair share of coughs, colds, and middle-ear infections. It should be remembered that the average normal child gets six or seven such infections every year, and so it is to be expected that there will be some who get infections almost every fortnight. Usually these infections are most frequent when the child first mixes with other children, such as on starting pre-school groups or classes and on entering school.

Typically the child has a runny nose, a fever, and a dry cough. It is very unusual for pneumonia to develop, and the cough is more likely to be the result of throat infection than chest infection. The child should always be examined by a doctor, particularly to check that the ears are not showing signs of a superimposed bacterial infection. If this is the case, the doctor may prescribe antibiotics. If the infection seems to be viral, antibiotics are of no use, and the condition will then clear up of its own accord, without any special treatment.

Relatively narrow air passages (ears, Eustachian tube, and nasal passages) cause some children to suffer more with these colds. A small number seem to have a continually runny nose. Such children should be examined to check that there is no foreign body (pea, pip, or other object) lodged in the nose. They should also be examined to see whether there is a polyp which needs to be removed. A polyp is a growth on the lining of the nose. Usually these are not present, and, with time, the nasal passages enlarge and these episodes become less frequent.

Parents sometimes ask if the nasal congestion will improve if the child is taken off cow's milk. Recent research has shown that this is not the case.

Glue ear

This is an important condition because it is a common and treatable cause of hearing-loss in children and adults with the syndrome. For this reason all children and adults with Down syndrome should have their hearing regularly tested.

Glue ear affects the middle ear, the part of the ear which lies behind the eardrum. There is a narrow passage, the Eustachian tube, which runs from the bottom of the middle ear to the back of the throat. It allows secretions produced by the lining of the middle ear to drain away, and air to enter and leave the middle ear.

If the Eustachian tube becomes blocked, fluid accumulates in the middle ear. This always has some effect on hearing. In some children, hearing loss is mild; but in others, it may be moderate or severe. In addition, the condition commonly gives rise to a 'blocked' feeling in the affected ear.

Glue ear can be transient, intermittent, or persistent (chronic). In most cases the cause is unknown. Infection of the middle ear may play an important role, particularly infection that has been only partially treated. Allergy is also often suspected as a cause; but it is difficult to be certain how prominent a role it plays. In some children, the adenoids (collections of lymphatic tissue that lie at the back of the throat) may be enlarged and cause obstruction to the Eustachian tube.

Glue ear is more common in children with Down syndrome, because they have narrow Eustachian tubes. As they grow, their Eustachian tubes enlarge, but always remain relatively narrow. This means that, while glue ear becomes less common after the age of ten years, it is still more common in adults with the syndrome than in other adults. Hearing should be regularly monitored, therefore, in both children and adults with the syndrome.

When glue ear is first detected, the child should be treated with an antibiotic for a period of four weeks. As it is impossible to know whether infection is playing a part, it seems reasonable to give all children a trial of an antibiotic to see whether the condition improves. In those children where allergy seems to be playing a part, that is, those with hay fever or other symptoms of allergy, the effects of anti-histamine and decongestant medicines should be tried. These should also be given for four weeks. Two weeks after a course of medicine, hearing should be re-tested. In those children in whom the condition resolves, no further treatment is needed, but hearing should be monitored every six months from then onward.

If, after a trial of medicine, the condition persists, referral to an ear, nose, and throat specialist should be arranged. The ear, nose, and throat specialist will examine the back of the throat, and make certain that there is no abnormality obstructing the Eustachian tube. An X-ray of the head may be needed, to see if the adenoids are enlarged. If this is the case, he or she may recommend that they should be removed (adenoidectomy).

In many cases, drainage of the middle ear will be recommended. This operation is carried out under a general anaesthetic. It takes a short while to perform, and the child can usually go home the same day. The procedure consists of making a small opening in the eardrum to allow fluid to escape and air to enter the middle ear. Because the hole would quickly close up, a tiny silicone tube (grommet) is inserted in the hole to keep it open. The grommet takes over the function of the Eustachian tube by providing a communication between the middle ear and the air outside.

After the operation, hearing usually improves, and children occasionally behave as if they are more comfortable. Parents sometimes report some improvement in their child's behaviour, attending skills, and language development. Hearing should always be tested after grommets have been inserted, as it may not have improved, or the improvement may be slight.

Grommets can become blocked (for example, by wax), and

so hearing must be monitored. Grommets usually remain in place for about six to twelve months, after which the body gets rid of them of its own accord. In some children, the condition recurs, and grommets must be reinserted.

Unrestricted swimming, bathing, and showering are not associated with an increased incidence of ear infection in children with grommets. Ear plugs need only be worn by the small number of children who experience discomfort when water enters their ears. The most effective ear plugs are those fashioned from silicone putty*.

It is important to remember that, if your child has glue ear, her hearing may be worse on some days than others. Always be sure to speak clearly to your child, and make certain that you gain her attention before giving an instruction. Request that she be allowed to sit near the front of the class so that she can hear the teacher.

Hearing-aids may be helpful in children with glue ear who continue to have moderate to severe hearing-loss, despite the insertion of grommets. It is very important that these are properly fitted, and that hearing is regularly checked both with and without the aids.

In some areas, there are itinerant support teachers for children with a hearing impairment, and you should enquire about the availability of such a teacher if your child has a significant hearing problem.

Eyes and vision

The vision of children with Down syndrome should be regularly checked, because there is a greater tendency for long-sightedness (hypermetropia) and short-sightedness (myopia) to develop.

Long-sightedness

Long-sightedness is more common, although usually milder than short-sightedness. Long-sightedness is associated with difficulties in seeing objects that are close by. Glasses need to be worn for close work, such as reading and writing.

---

* Available under the trade names: 'Physicians' Choice' (U.K.) and 'Surgipac' (Australia).

Short-sightedness

Short-sightedness is usually indicated by the child's need to get very close up to objects. Children who sit close to the television set, however, do not necessarily do so because they are short-sighted. They often do this because they enjoy being close to the action. Short-sightedness is corrected by glasses, which usually need to be worn as much as possible. Holes can be drilled in the parts of the glasses that lie just behind the ears, and a broad elasticized band can be attached which wraps around the back of the head, keeping the glasses in place. Glasses with curled wire ends that fit around the ears may be sufficient. If the child takes the glasses off, you should not make a fuss, but say firmly 'No', and replace them. Some children will not tolerate glasses except when at school. In this case, it may be best to have the teacher keep the glasses, which can be put on on arrival and taken off before going home.

Squint

A squint is the medical term for cross-eyes. This is different from the more colloquial use, meaning to 'screw-up' the eyes when looking at something. Squints are more common in children with Down syndrome.

In squinting, eyes may either go out of alignment every now and again, or may always be crossed. In Down syndrome, the squint is usually a convergent squint, with both eyes turned inwards towards the nose. When a child's eyes are crossed, she cannot use both eyes simultaneously without seeing double, as the two eyes are looking at different objects. The brain, therefore, ignores what one of the eyes is looking at, and this is what is sometimes known as 'lazy eye'. If this is allowed to continue, the lazy eye will eventually lose its vision because of lack of use. This will leave the person with only one good eye, making her vulnerable to any damage to that eye. It also takes away the advantages of seeing with both eyes, which are a better perception of depth, a wider field of vision, and a greater ability to notice objects against a background.

A number of children under the age of four months have an intermittent squint, and this is of no consequence. At this young age, the eyes are not yet well controlled by the brain, and may not function as a unit from time to time. But any child with a persistent squint, or an intermittent squint after the age of four months, should be seen by an ophthalmologist.

If the child is using one eye and then the other, this is referred to as 'alternating fixation'. If the child freely alternates from one eye to the other, nothing may need to be done. If, however, only one eye is being used consistently, glasses may be needed, or the better eye may need to be covered by an eye patch for a period each day to encourage the other eye to be used. For children who refuse to wear a patch, the ophthalmologist may prescribe atropine eye-drops, which temporarily blur vision in the better eye.

Squints can be operated on to correct the alignment of the eyes. This is important not only for the child's vision, but also for her appearance. A squint operation is performed under general anaesthetic, and takes approximately an hour or two. During the operation, the eyes are repositioned by realigning the eye muscles situated around the eyeball. Most children can go home the same day, but will have some pain, redness, and swelling of the eyes for a few days after the procedure. In about a third of children who have a squint operation, a second operation is required later to make further adjustments to the position of the eyes.

Nystagmus

This is another eye condition that is more common in children with Down syndrome. It occurs when the brain does not accurately control the movement of the muscles around the eye ball. Instead of remaining steady when the child looks at an object, the eyes jerk to and fro at a rapid rate. This condition is sometimes slightly improved by the prescription of glasses; but it is usually not amenable to treatment. The continual movement of the eyes reduces the visual ability of the child; but this is generally not as great a reduction as might be supposed by someone who is watching the eyes move.

Cataracts

Clouding of the lens (cataract) may occur in Down syndrome. The commonest form consists of small flakes at the edge of the lens, which usually do not interfere with vision. Rarely, cataracts are dense, and do interfere with vision, in which case they should be removed surgically. Thick glasses are then needed, although lens implants can now be inserted in some adolescents and adults.

Keratoconus

This is a condition where the cornea (the transparent membrane in the front of the eyeball) assumes a conical shape. It is more common in people with Down syndrome, but is usually very mild when present. The associated visual disturbance is usually corrected by glasses, although some individuals may need to wear hard contact lenses. Very rarely, the condition worsens, and vision can only be corrected by a corneal graft. Keratoconus usually progresses most rapidly in late adolescence and early adulthood, before stabilizing.

Muscles, bones, and joints

Children with Down syndrome often have very mobile joints, which give them the appearance of being 'double-jointed'. This, like their low tone, diminishes with age, and is far less noticeable after the age of ten years.

The low muscle tone and mobile joints of children with Down syndrome mean that some parts of the body may be held in abnormal positions. If this happens occasionally, it is of no concern; but if limbs are held for long periods of time in certain abnormal positions, the bones may assume an abnormal shape as the child grows.

Try to stop your young baby with Down syndrome from sleeping for long periods with the feet twisted inwards underneath her (Fig. 15). Otherwise later, when she walks, her feet may be turned in.

Because of low tone, children with Down syndrome often sit in a W-position (Fig. 16). Held for long periods of time, this position causes the thigh bone (femur) to twist inward. If your child spends long periods in this position, encourage her rather to sit with legs crossed or straight out in front of her.

Low tone also makes children with Down syndrome more likely to have flat feet. In the past, too much was made of flat feet. About one in five normal people has flat feet, and these rarely cause any problem to them. (High arches are more troublesome!) Flat feet, like other low-tone problems, get better with time. Supports, special shoes, and exercises are of questionable value.

Fig. 15. Incorrect lying position.

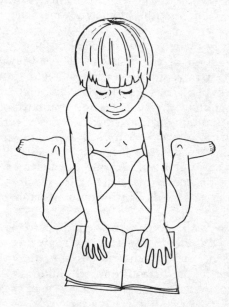

Fig. 16. W-sitting position.

The neck

The top two neck bones (vertebrae) that lie just below the skull are called the atlas and the axis. The joint between them is called the atlanto-axial joint. It has now been established that in about 10–20 per cent of children and adults with Down syndrome, there is increased mobility of this joint. This is known as atlanto-axial instability. Atlanto-axial instability is important

only because it can lead to dislocation of the two bones. This
dislocation occurs when the atlas slides forward over the axis.
The spinal cord can then become compressed by a bony projec-
tion of the axis (the odontoid process), and can be damaged.
This can cause paralysis of the limbs, and interfere with other
bodily functions, such as breathing and bladder-control. This
dislocation is usually a gradual process, taking many months or
years; but it can happen suddenly. Excessive movements of
the neck in any direction increase the chance of dislocation
occurring.

It is important to realize that laxity of the atlanto-axial joint
is not directly related to the degree of laxity in other joints, and
may occur in children with Down syndrome whose other joints
are not particularly mobile.

The only way to detect atlanto-axial instability before it has
led to compression of the spinal cord is by an X-ray of the
neck. This must be a side view (lateral), and should be taken
with the neck bent forwards (in flexion) and backwards (in
extension). The flexion view is the more important, as it shows
the maximum amount of movement of the atlanto-axial joint.
In children who are very distressed at having an X-ray, this
view is all that is needed. The radiologist assesses the amount of
mobility of the joint by measuring the distance between the
axis and atlas on the X-ray plate (atlanto-odontoid distance)
when the neck is flexed. This should normally be less than
4mm.

All children with Down syndrome should have an annual
examination by a doctor to detect any signs of compression of
the spinal cord, such as changes in the strength, tone, and
reflexes in the limbs. In addition, all children who engage in
activities which put stress on the neck (some of these were listed
earlier in this chapter) should have the neck X-rayed at about
three to four years of age (or earlier if the child will be engaging
in any of these activities at a younger age). For the purposes of
management, each child will fall into one of the following three
groups:

1. Normal X-ray and no abnormality on examination

This is the largest group, into which 80–90 per cent of children
with Down syndrome fall. If your child is in this group, you
do not have to take any special precautions. She can take part in
the activities listed earlier in this chapter.

It is still not known whether atlanto-axial instability, if absent in a child at four years, will develop later. In view of our lack of knowledge at the present time, it seems wise to do a second X-ray of the neck on all children in this group when they reach ten years of age.

2. Abnormal X-ray but no abnormality on examination

These children have an atlanto-odontoid distance of greater than 4mm on X-ray, and therefore have atlanto-axial instability. But examination by a doctor reveals no signs of compression of the spinal cord. About 10–20 per cent of children with Down syndrome fall into this group.

If your child falls into this group, she should not engage in the activities listed earlier, as they may cause spinal-cord compression. Instead, she can be encouraged to take part in other sports, such as swimming, slow horse-riding, and running. She should always wear a seat-belt, and have a head-support when travelling in a car. If she needs a general anaesthetic, the anaesthetist should be alerted to the presence of atlanto-axial instability, so that he or she can take appropriate precautions when extending the head to insert a breathing tube.

A child in this group should be examined every six months for signs of cord compression, and have her neck X-rayed annually. Fortunately, the majority of children in this group will not develop any signs of cord compression. Those who do, should be managed in the same manner as those in the following group.

3. Abnormal X-ray and abnormalities on examination

Only one in a hundred children with Down syndrome falls into this group. There is a danger that the spinal-cord compression will worsen, and it is recommended that such children undergo surgery in order to fuse the back of the atlas to the back of the axis. This will reduce the mobility of the neck as a whole, but prevents life-threatening dislocation of the atlanto-axial joint. Other suggested treatments, such as the wearing of neck collars and neck-muscle strengthening exercises, are not helpful. The latter may even precipitate dislocation.

The skin

Many children with Down syndrome have dry skin, which may flake, crack, or itch. The following measures may help: Put some bicarbonate of soda in the bath (a handful in a half-filled bath). Try not to use soap, as it removes the skin's natural oils. If the child is clearly dirty, soap may be necessary; but usually a rinse is sufficient until puberty. Do not put oil in the bath, as it stops the water from penetrating and moisturizing the skin. Allow the bath water to hydrate the skin, and then seal the water in by rubbing an oily substance into the skin after the bath while the skin is still wet. The best substance for this purpose is Sorbolene with 10 per cent Glycerine, which can be bought in bulk from chemists and some supermarkets. It can be rubbed all over the body, including the face (with care not to get it into the eyes). If itchy skin or a rash persists, the advice of your doctor should be sought.

The teeth

The teeth of children with Down syndrome erupt later than those of normal children. This means that they tend to keep their deciduous (milk) teeth for longer than usual, with more resulting wear and tear. In some children, these teeth can become quite worn down with time. In addition, research has shown that children with the syndrome are more susceptible to gum disease. It is, therefore, important to pay attention to your child's dental care. This is particularly so in children who have heart disease, for reasons that will be discussed in the next chapter.

Your child should visit the dentist once a year from the age of two. Avoid excessive sugar in your child's diet, and give her fluoride supplements if fluoride is not already added to your drinking water.

You should start brushing your child's teeth from the time her first tooth appears. Flossing of teeth is difficult in most young children with Down syndrome, because of their small mouths. But flossing is important, because of the increased incidence of gum disease, and should be attempted from about six years of age. When brushing your child's teeth, use a brush with a small head and medium nylon bristles. Use only a speck of toothpaste, as often much of it is swallowed. Teeth can be successfully cleaned without toothpaste. Position your child with her back to you, her head and shoulders leaning against your chest. You can then tilt her head up and see into her mouth. When cleaning the front and back of each tooth, hold the brush at a 45-degree angle to the gum, and jiggle it gently. A scrubbing motion should only be used when cleaning the biting surfaces.

Older children can often learn to brush their own teeth, but should be supervised. Children who have difficulty controlling a toothbrush may be helped by an electric toothbrush.

The thyroid gland

The thyroid gland is situated in the front of the neck, and produces thyroid hormone which it secretes into the blood. The amount of thyroid hormone in the blood must be maintained within specific limits, or certain body functions will become disordered. Insufficient thyroid hormone in the blood is known as hypothyroidism (*hypo* = below). Hypothyroidism may be present at birth (congenital), or develop later (acquired). Both forms are more common in individuals with Down syndrome than in the general population.

Hypothyroidism is a difficult condition to recognize in the early stages. This is particularly the case in individuals with Down syndrome, because hypothyroidism and Down syndrome share a number of features. It is for this reason that a regular blood test to detect hypothyroidism is recommended in all children and adults with the syndrome.

The cause, presentation, and consequences of the two forms of hypothyroidism differ, and they will therefore be discussed separately.

1. Congenital hypothyroidism

This form of hypothyroidism is approximately thirty times more common in new-borns with Down syndrome than in the rest of the population, occurring in about one in a hundred and fifty new-borns with the syndrome. It may be due to failure of the thyroid gland to develop in the fetus; or, if the gland is present, it may be incapable of manufacturing or secreting the hormone.

Early detection and treatment of hypothyroidism at birth is more important than at any other time of life. This is because the brain continues to develop during the first two years of life, and insufficient thyroid hormone during this period can result in permanent intellectual impairment. For the child with Down syndrome, untreated congenital hypothyroidism will give rise to a greater degree of intellectual disability than would have occurred as a result of Down syndrome alone.

Congenital hypothyroidism is seldom apparent at birth. When signs do appear, after a few months, they are often so similar to some of the features of Down syndrome that the hypothyroidism may go undetected. Signs of hypothyroidism at this time include poor feeding, constipation, a hoarse cry, and sleepiness. The muscle tone is lowered, and development delayed.

In many countries, all new-borns have their blood tested, at or shortly after birth, to detect those with hypothyroidism. If you live in an area where this is not the routine practice, make sure that your child does have the test as soon as possible after birth.

In a small number of infants with congenital hypothyroidism, the amount of thyroid hormone in the blood may be within the normal range at birth, but then falls over the subsequent months as the thyroid gland becomes depleted. It is for this reason that repeat tests at six and twelve months have been recommended.

Treatment of congenital hypothyroidism is by the oral administration of the missing hormone. This treatment will need to continue for life. The longer congenital hypothyroidism remains untreated, the greater the degree of irreversible intellectual impairment.

2. Acquired hypothyroidism

This form of the disorder affects as many as one in five adults with Down syndrome, and about half as many children. It is due to a disease known as Hashimoto thyroiditis (inflammation of the thyroid gland), named after a Japanese surgeon, Dr H. Hashimoto (1881–1934). At one time it was thought that this disease was confined to adults; however, this is not the case. Children with Down syndrome as young as one year of age have been reported with the condition. This is why annual thyroid tests should be carried out during childhood as well as adulthood.

Hashimoto thyroiditis comes about when the body makes antibodies against the thyroid gland. The reason why the body starts treating part of itself as foreign is unknown. The antibodies circulate in the blood and slowly destroy the gland, so that the level of thyroid hormone in the blood decreases.

Hashimoto thyroiditis is not confined to Down syndrome. It is the commonest cause of acquired hypothyroidism in those without the syndrome as well.

The onset of hypothyroidism in Hashimoto thyroiditis is usually so insidious that the changes frequently go unnoticed by those in regular contact with the affected individual. The early symptoms are very variable. In children, the first sign is often poor growth. In adults, weakness, dry coarse skin, lethargy, puffiness about the eyes, constipation, memory impairment, and intolerance of cold weather are among the more common signs. Many of these signs are often present in people with Down syndrome without hypothyroidism, making recognition of the condition without a blood test difficult. If these early signs are missed, and the condition is allowed to progress untreated, serious complications, such as heart disease and mental disturbance, can develop.

In hypothyroidism that starts after the age of about two years, all changes resolve with oral administration of thyroid hormone. Treatment will need to continue throughout life. The treatment should not be stopped, as this will cause a drop in the blood thyroid-hormone level, and may precipitate the onset of life-threatening complications.

It must be emphasized that, while hypothyroidism is more common in Down syndrome, and shares some of its features, the two conditions are separate entities. There was a time in the nineteenth century when some physicians believed that Down syndrome was caused by thyroid deficiency. This is not the case. Most people with the syndrome have normal thyroid gland function. The practice of giving thyroid hormone to children and adults with Down syndrome in the absence of hypothyroidism is inappropriate, and not without danger. Not only will the features of Down syndrome remain unchanged, but the extra hormone in the blood can give rise to thyroid-hormone toxicity.

The intestines

Duodenal atresia

This condition is present at birth in about 10–15 per cent of infants with Down syndrome. In duodenal atresia there is narrowing of the first part of the small intestine (the duodenum).

This means that food cannot pass through the intestine after leaving the stomach. The condition causes problems during the new-born period. Vomiting usually occurs within a few hours after birth, and the upper part of the stomach becomes distended. The condition is usually diagnosed by an X-ray of the abdomen. Duodenal atresia is treated by an operation in which the obstructed section of the intestine is removed and the duodenum joined up again.

Hirschsprung disease

This condition is less common than duodenal atresia, but also occurs more frequently in children with Down syndrome than in normal children. It is named after Dr H. Hirschsprung, a Danish doctor (1830–1916). The condition is due to a lack of certain nerves in the wall of the rectum, and sometimes in part of the large intestine. This means that the normal pulsating movements that push the food through the rectum do not occur properly. This causes constipation, usually in the new-born period or in infancy. The abdomen becomes distended, and vomiting may follow. Initial treatment is by an operation allowing the abnormal segment of the intestine to be bypassed. A hole (colostomy) is made in the abdomen, through which faeces can be excreted into a disposable bag or nappy. The colostomy is later closed, the abnormal segment of the intestine removed, and the intestine rejoined, to allow faeces to be passed through the anus.

Constipation

Constipation is a common problem in children with Down syndrome. It is related partly to the low tone of the abdominal muscles, which does not allow sufficient pressure to develop inside the abdomen when the child tries to pass a motion. It is important to make certain that when your child sits on the toilet seat, her feet are in contact with the floor. If the child's legs are too short to reach the floor, a low step or seat should be placed under each foot to give her something to push against. Take toilet training slowly, with little fuss, and do not keep the child for more than ten or fifteen minutes on the potty or toilet, as this encourages negativity. If constipation does occur, your doctor should be consulted. Treatment with laxatives may be needed for a period. The role of fibre in the diet is also important. Replace refined grains and grain-products, such as white flour, white rice, and white pasta with whole-grain equivalents, and encourage your child to eat more fruit and vegetables.

Rarely, a mild form of Hirschsprung disease may not give rise to any problems until after infancy, when it causes constipation. This is why all constipated children should have an examination which includes the doctor inserting a finger into the anus to check for this condition. In all constipated children with Down syndrome, thyroid hormone deficiency should also be excluded.

Leukaemia

Leukaemia, although more common in children with Down syndrome than in other children, affects only about one child in a hundred with the syndrome. It usually becomes apparent by skin pallor, easy bleeding, or bone pain. Blood tests will then reveal abnormal growth of white blood cells.

With modern treatment, leukaemia can always be brought under control, so that the child will remain well for a period. In over half the children, the disease can be permanently cured.

Klinefelter syndrome

About one in a hundred boys with Down syndrome has an extra X chromosome in addition to the extra number 21 chromosome. This means that the boy, in addition to Down syndrome, has a condition known as Klinefelter syndrome (named after Dr H. F. Klinefelter, a U.S. physician). The presence of Klinefelter syndrome will be detected by the same chromosome test that confirms the diagnosis of Down syndrome. Boys with Klinefelter syndrome in addition to Down syndrome will have relatively small testes (testicles), and not undergo the normal development of the body during adolescence. Infertility is the rule in this condition. Boys with Klinefelter syndrome may need to be treated with male sex-hormone during adolescence, in order to develop the normal physical changes of puberty.

7. The heart

About one-third of children with Down syndrome will be born with a heart abnormality. It is important to realize that the heart defects of Down syndrome are already present at birth. If no defect is found on thorough examination of your child's heart at six weeks of age, you can be confident that your child is one of the two-thirds of children who have no heart problem. *If so, this chapter will not concern you.*

Parents of children who do have a heart defect usually have many questions about their child's condition, and so I shall describe in some detail aspects of heart disease in children with Down syndrome.

HOW THE HEART WORKS

You will more easily understand the different kinds of heart defects, and their effects on the body, if you know how the normal heart works.

The heart is a pump. It pumps blood through two circuits. One circuit takes blood through the lungs, the other through the rest of the body. In the lungs, the blood receives oxygen from the air. It then returns to the heart and is pumped to the rest of the body, where it gives up this oxygen so that it can be used by the cells. When blood leaves the lungs, it is pink in colour. Once the blood has given up its oxygen to the rest of the body, it turns blue.

The heart contains four chambers (Fig. 17). Two smaller upper chambers act as receiving chambers (the atria). The one on the child's left receives oxygenated (pink) blood from the lungs, the one on the right, spent (blue) blood from the rest of the body. Each atrium leads to a large pumping chamber (ventricle) below it. Valves between each atrium and its corresponding ventricle allow blood to pass from atrium to ventricle but not back again. The valve between the right atrium and the right ventricle is called the tricuspid valve, that between the left atrium and left ventricle, the mitral valve.

When the heart contracts (squeezes), the process occurs in

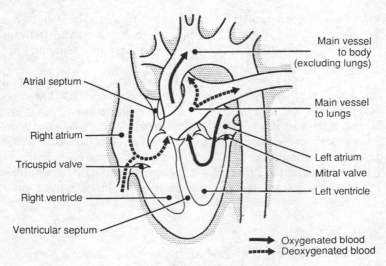

Fig. 17. Normal heart.

two steps: First, the atria contract, emptying blood into the corresponding ventricles. Then the ventricles contract strongly, pumping blood to the lungs (in the case of the right ventricle) and the rest of the body (in the case of the left). The left ventricle must pump more strongly, as blood leaving it must reach every part of the body. It is, therefore, a larger, more muscular chamber than the right ventricle, which only has to pump blood to the nearby lungs.

The walls between the two atria and the two ventricles are called the atrial septum and ventricular septum respectively. These are normally effective barriers, that prevent the mixing of blue blood from the right side of the heart with pink blood from the left.

TYPES OF HEART DISORDER IN DOWN SYNDROME

If heart disease is present, it can take a number of different forms. These are described below:

Atrio-ventricular septal defect (A-VSD)

This is the most common heart defect in Down syndrome, and is present in one in six children.

In an atrio-ventricular septal defect there is a hole between the two atria, and, in some cases, between the two ventricles as well. In addition, the valves between the atria and ventricles are usually malformed.

This defect was commonly referred to as an 'endocardial cushion defect' in the past, because it was believed that mal-development of structures called the 'endocardial cushions' played a part in its causation. Recent work has cast doubt on this theory, and so the descriptive term 'atrio-ventricular septal defect' is preferable.

Atrio-ventricular septal defects may be partial or complete. The two forms are equally common in children with Down syndrome.

Partial A-VSD

This was also known as an 'ostium primum defect'; however, this term is inaccurate, and is no longer used. In this form of A-VSD, the ventricular septum is intact, but there is a hole between left and right atria. In addition, there is usually an abnormality of the mitral valve, allowing blood to leak back into the left atrium when the left ventricle contracts.

Many children with this defect initially have no symptoms of heart disease. But the heart cannot usually cope with the leak of blood through the hole and the valve, and eventually breath-lessness, easy tiring, and frequent chest infections occur. For this reason, surgery to close the hole and repair the valve is usually advised at about two to four years.

Complete A-VSD

This is the more severe form of atrio-ventricular septal defect. The atrial and ventricular septa are malformed, as are the mitral and tricuspid valves. This defect is also known as a common atrio-ventricular canal (AV canal).

Initially, because the left ventricle contracts more powerfully than the right, blood crosses the centre of the heart from left ventricle to right. The lungs therefore receive blood from both sides of the heart, making them congested and stiff. Breathing becomes difficult, and the baby tires easily, especially when sucking. Babies with this condition often fail to gain weight.

The baby with these symptoms may improve if given digita-lis, a medicine which slows the racing heart, and makes it pump more effectively. Diuretics, medicines which increase the amount of urine, also help rid the lungs of some of their extra fluid. The infant will usually feel better if kept in a sitting position, and such babies often sleep happily sitting in an infant chair. If feeding continues to be difficult, a tube may need to be passed down into the stomach. This relieves the infant of the work of sucking. His formula may need to be strengthened to help him gain weight.

The current approach to the management of a complete A-VSD is to operate during infancy to repair the defect completely.

Ventricular septal defect (VSD)

This is the most common heart defect in children who do not have Down syndrome. In children with the syndrome, it occurs in approximately one in ten children.

A hole is present between the two ventricles. This may be very small, causing no problems to the child. Slightly larger holes usually do cause problems. Some of the blood in the stronger left ventricle crosses the hole, enters the right ventricle, and is pumped into the lungs. This means that the lungs have an increased amount of blood, which makes them congested and stiff. Breathlessness, poor feeding, and resulting failure to gain weight during infancy follow. The infant may be helped by being sat up, and by medicine for heart failure as described for a complete A-VSD (see above). Tube-feeding may be necessary.

In some children, the VSD becomes smaller as the heart grows. Some small holes may close of their own accord. This sort of improvement is usually seen towards the end of the first year, and the breathlessness, poor weight-gain, and repeated chest infections become less marked.

In the case of a small to medium-sized hole which is getting smaller, the decision about an operation may be deferred until just before starting school. In some children, an operation may never be necessary.

In children with large holes, there is more risk of irreversible damage occurring in the lung vessels in response to the increased blood flow through them. There is therefore more urgency to close the hole. It is for this reason that complete repair of such a VSD during infancy is now the preferred treatment.

Patent ductus arteriosus (PDA)

A patent ductus arteriosus is the third most common heart defect in children with Down syndrome, occurring in about one in fifty children with the syndrome.

When the fetus is in the womb, its circulation is adapted to very special circumstances. Oxygen is obtained from the mother's blood via the placenta. The lungs are not in use, and so little blood passes through them. There is a special large vessel (duct) that allows blood to be diverted away from the unused lungs straight to the vessels supplying the rest of the body. Once the child is born, a process of adaptation takes place over a few hours, and this duct, no longer of use, closes up forever.

The condition of a patent (open) ductus arteriosus occurs when the duct fails to close after birth. The higher blood-pressure that normally exists in the vessels leading to the body, compared with those going to the lungs, means that some blood bound for the body leaks back through the duct into the vessels taking blood to the lungs. The lungs become stiff from excess blood passing through, and breathlessness, poor feeding, and chest infections may occur if the duct is large.

Closure of the duct is usually easy. The heart itself does not need to be opened, as the duct lies above it. All that is needed is for an opening to be made in the side of the chest, and for the duct to be tied shut.

Eisenmenger complex

This is the name given to the complication that develops in children (and adults) with certain types of heart disease once the resistance to blood flow in the lung vessels has become very high, and the vessels have irreversibly narrowed. This may occur in a child who has an A-VSD, VSD, or PDA if these cannot be repaired in time.

This complication is not always avoidable. Some children, for reasons we do not understand, have a lung circulation that develops high resistance to blood flow early in infancy. Others may be so weakened by heart failure during infancy and early childhood that the underlying defect cannot be repaired in time to avoid irreversibly high resistance developing in the lung vessels. In cases where children can be operated on before this occurs, Eisenmenger complex will not usually develop. Once Eisenmenger complex has developed, surgical treatment can no longer be performed.

The symptoms of Eisenmenger complex are similar whatever the predisposing heart defect. With increased pressure in the lungs, the amount of blood able to pass through them decreases. Initially, as the resistance in the lung vessels rises, the child's condition may improve. The breathlessness and failure to thrive associated with the underlying condition may resolve, as the lungs are no longer so full of blood and so stiff. But as the blood pressure in the lungs increases, blue blood, low in oxygen, will be forced from the right side of the heart to the left through the A-VSD, VSD, or PDA. The child then begins to look blue (cyanosed).

Initially, this blueness (cyanosis) is mild, and the child may remain well for many years. The only early symptom may be a tendency to breathlessness and fatigue on strenuous exertion. The child's condition can deteriorate quickly, however, and certain precautions should be taken. Any infection must be treated promptly, and ample fluids should always be made available, as dehydration can cause the child's condition to deteriorate. Women with Eisenmenger complex should not take oral contraceptives, as these can make the condition worse. Care must be taken if a person with this complex needs an anaesthetic.

With time, the cyanosis increases, and the body tries to compensate for the reduced amount of oxygen in the blood by making more red blood corpuscles, to carry as much oxygen as possible. This does not totally compensate for the reduced oxygen, and, in addition, causes the blood to thicken and flow sluggishly. This may make it necessary to remove some blood and replace it with clear fluid (partial exchange transfusion).

Some people with Eisenmenger complex can remain fairly well until their twenties or thirties. Eventually, the heart can no longer pump effectively against the resistance of the lung vessels. Unfortunately, this form of heart failure usually responds poorly to medicines.

Tetralogy of Fallot

Approximately one in a hundred children with Down syndrome has this particular group of heart abnormalities, named after Dr Fallot (1850–1911). The word 'tetralogy' describes four abnormalities which occur together. The two important ones are a large hole in the ventricular septum (a VSD) and a narrowing of the blood-vessel leading from the heart to the lungs. As a result of these defects, blood ejected from the ventricles mixes in the area of the VSD before entering the two overlying vessels. Only a small amount of blood manages to force its way to the lungs. Most takes the path of least resistance to the rest of the body.

The amount of blue blood going to the body changes with any variation in the narrowing of the vessel to the lungs. With time, this degree of narrowing varies in a way that is not completely understood.

When a baby is born with Fallot tetralogy, he may already be blue; however, some babies with the condition are a normal colour (acyanotic Fallot), and only become blue by two to four years of age. Blueness may then be constant, or may only appear in 'blue spells' (cyanotic attacks). Some children may have blue spells with fever, or when they have a very hot bath. Often there is no apparent precipitating event.

Children with this condition may spontaneously take up a squatting position after exertion. Sitting with knees held up against the chest causes a rise in resistance to blood travelling from the heart to the lower limbs. More blood is thus forced through the lungs, correcting slightly for the lack of oxygen.

During a persistent cyanotic episode, you should put your child in a squatting position and try to comfort him. He should be taken to hospital, where he can be given oxygen to breathe, and injections if needed. To avoid episodes, fevers should be treated promptly, by keeping the child cool and giving him paracetamol. Children with Fallot tetralogy should not have very hot baths.

The body eventually responds to the presence of less oxygen in the blood by making more red blood cells (see the section on the Eisenmenger complex above). This has the side-effect of making the blood flow sluggishly. It is therefore important that children who are blue from Fallot tetralogy get as much fluid to drink as they want, and that they are not allowed to become dehydrated when ill. They should also be given adequate iron supplements, as the rapid production of red blood cells uses extra amounts of this mineral.

Once cyanosis develops, surgery must be considered. Complete repair of Fallot tetralogy is a complex open-heart operation. If successful, the child becomes a normal colour, and can tolerate moderate exercise.

If complete repair must be deferred, and cyanosis is a problem, a graft can be inserted to allow blood to bypass the obstruction at the base of the vessel to the lungs, thus reducing blueness. This is a relatively easy procedure, and can be repeated should the graft become blocked.

Occasionally, a medicine called propranolol (Inderal) is used to keep symptoms under control prior to an operation. It needs to be taken regularly by mouth, and may then reduce the number of blue attacks, or prevent them completely.

PREVENTION OF ENDOCARDITIS

Precautions should be taken when a child with any of the heart defects mentioned above has an operation, particularly in an area where bacteria are present. These areas include the mouth (dental manipulations such as extraction or drilling) and the bladder (urological procedures). Such operations may allow bacteria to enter the blood stream. If there is a heart defect, the abnormal blood flow through the heart may encourage bacteria to multiply, and cause an infection within the heart (endocarditis). To prevent this, antibiotics should be given one hour before such procedures to kill these bacteria as soon as they enter the bloodstream. Antibiotics should not be given too long before the procedure, or resistant strains of bacteria will have time to develop. The best way to avoid the need for dental procedures is by regular dental checks, and conscientious flossing and cleaning of teeth.

8. Your child's behaviour

Two statements are often made about the behaviour of children and adults with Down syndrome. One is that they are placid individuals who are easy to manage. The other is that they are strong-willed and difficult to control. The co-existence of two such conflicting views reflects the real truth about the behaviour of people with Down syndrome—namely, that it varies markedly from one person to another. Some are placid, some determined, and many fall temperamentally somewhere between these two extremes. While some parents find their children with Down syndrome easier to control than their normal children, others have to cope with a wide range of behaviour problems.

ARE THERE SPECIAL BEHAVIOUR PROBLEMS ASSOCIATED WITH DOWN SYNDROME?

Children with Down syndrome reach each stage in their development later than the average child. They are therefore older and physically bigger than normal children when at the same behavioural age. Two-year-old tantrums, for example, may only occur in a child with Down syndrome when she reaches four years. The behaviour may then be more disruptive because the child is larger. Such behaviour in an older child may puzzle observers. There are, however, no behaviour problems unique to children with Down syndrome. Problems, when they occur, are generally similar to those seen in normal children of a younger age, and are usually amenable to simple methods of behaviour modification.

WHAT IS BEHAVIOUR MODIFICATION?

Many parents practise behaviour modification without realizing it. They do this by rewarding their child for good behaviour and punishing her for bad. Some parents need help in order to do this in the most effective way. Children benefit from knowing where they stand, and being able to direct their energies into more constructive and rewarding activities. Behaviour modification is a form of teaching, employed in situations where explanation alone does not succeed.

Identify the behaviour

The first step in a behaviour modification programme is to observe your child's behaviour and identify the behaviour you want to change. You need to avoid general statements about your child such as 'she is impossible', and instead focus on specific things she does which worry or annoy you, for instance, running away from you when out shopping.

What kind of behaviour is it?

A behaviour is an action or series of actions which you can observe. There are two kinds of behaviour: good behaviour, which you want to encourage, and undesirable behaviour, which you want to get rid of. Ideally, it is best to teach a child useful skills to replace unwanted behaviour. I will therefore first describe how you might encourage desirable behaviour which can then be rewarded.

Encouraging good behaviour so that it can be rewarded

One way of encouraging good behaviour is to demonstrate the behaviour to the child in the hope that she will imitate it. Some children seem to be more keen to imitate behaviour than others. Your child may copy the parent she identifies with more strongly, and you should take advantage of this. For example, if you want your son to start passing urine into the toilet, it might be an idea for his father to demonstrate this, mentioning that this is how 'big boys' do it.

Children also tend to copy other children. If you want your child to use the potty, try to let her see other children doing this, in the hope that she may imitate them.

Another way of encouraging good behaviour is by putting the child in a position that would facilitate this. In the case of potty training, this might be by actually putting the child on the potty and gently keeping her there, provided she is not distressed.

Another technique is to give the child an instruction such as 'make a poo'. This sort of prompt has to be short and comprehensible to the child.

Of course, all of these methods can be combined.

If, as sometimes happens, the correct behaviour suddenly occurs, you should take advantage of this and reward the child immediately. Be alert to 'catch' your child demonstrating a good behaviour, so that this can be rewarded.

Rewarding good behaviour

How should you reward your child? The simplest sort of reward would be to praise what the child has done by making a fuss, smiling, and saying, 'well done' or 'good dry bed' or 'good walking', etc. Note that 'good' is used to describe the behaviour, not the child. This emphasizes what it is that you are praising, and does not in any way reflect on the child's worth. These simple verbal rewards should always be given, and are often more powerful than parents realize. In some cases, however, they are not enough on their own. The older the child, the less likely it is that this simple kind of reward will suffice. In this case, you need to provide some tangible reward. This may take the form of a star on a chart, a 'smiley' stamp on the hand, a sweet, a raisin, a special toy, or an outing. In more sophisticated children, it may be necessary to have a system where a specific number of small tokens earns something a little larger. Beware of the trap of making the reward too big or expensive. You should not make it too easy to get big rewards, although you should make it reasonably easy to earn lesser rewards to encourage the child.

The reward system should be carefully planned before it is explained to the child. Stamps, tokens, or charts should be available at the outset. Once the behaviour modification programme is in operation, you will need to revise the reward system if it is clear that the child is waiting too long for a reward or is getting too many rewards.

Keep up this tangible reward system until the child loses interest, which she will invariably do once the desired behaviour has been established for a period of time. Do keep up the praise, however, even when tangible rewards are no longer given.

Discouraging undesirable behaviour

Discouraging undesirable behaviour causes parents much difficulty and confusion. Without realizing it, they are often rewarding the bad behaviour, and doing exactly the opposite of what they mean to do; or they are using an ineffective way of getting rid of the unwanted behaviour.

Ways that do not work

How can you discourage an unwanted behaviour? The most common method is to scold the child or argue with her. Most parents would agree that this is not usually successful. The reason for this is that, for many children, any attention from their parents acts as a reward. Children thrive on attention, and always seem to want more. They prefer praise; but any attention, even scolding, can be rewarding for a child.

Some parents resort to slapping their child, but often find that this does not help. This may make parents very distressed, as they regard this as the most extreme action they can take. The reason why slapping does not seem to work is probably because it *is* such an extreme thing to do. Although it is unpleasant for the child, it is also unpleasant for the parent, and most children realize this. After the slap, parents invariably feel a bit guilty; whereas the pain caused by the slap has subsided, and the child may enjoy the sympathy she senses from the remorseful parent. Slapping may therefore work for the moment, but usually does not eradicate a recurrent behaviour.

Ways that work

What then can parents do when these traditional methods do not work? The first thing that parents need to learn is to do nothing. Children thrive on attention, even in the form of shouting and slapping. By withholding attention, many behaviours will diminish or disappear. Ignoring behaviour is a difficult thing to do. In fact, it is questionable whether parents can ever completely ignore their child's behaviour. You can, however, *pretend to ignore the behaviour*. To do this, you have to stifle your natural responses, avoid making eye contact with the child, and look calm. Busy yourself with some activity unrelated to the child, and refuse to become involved in any discussion or argument about the behaviour which you are trying to get rid of. When the child has stopped demonstrating the particular behaviour, invite her to take part in what you are doing and resume normal conversation with her. Do not show annoyance once you start interacting with her again.

In some cases, it is impossible to ignore your child's behaviour. She may be so active and destructive, or possibly aggressive, that you cannot pretend to ignore her because of your concern that she may injure herself or damage something. You may be so angry with her that you are afraid of losing control and harming her. In such situations, you have to remove her to a place where she can no longer receive the reward of your attention.

This technique is known as 'time-out', and consists of gently taking her and putting her in an environment away from your company. The aim of using 'time-out' is not to create discomfort or fear in the child, but simply to remove her from the place where she is receiving reinforcement for what she is doing. Usually the most convenient place for 'time-out' is the child's bedroom. Leave her there until you have both calmed down. While the child is there, any shouting or screaming should be ignored. It is important not to take the child out until she has quietened down, otherwise she may get the idea that she is being taken out because of her screaming and shouting. You can either tell the child in a calm voice that you will not take her out until she is quiet or, if she does not understand this and will not co-operate, you can wait until there is a pause in her crying and then take her out. Some children are so destructive in their own rooms that it may be necessary to pick another room in the house. Concern is sometimes expressed that, if a child spends 'time-out' in her bedroom, she will develop a bad association with it. In practice, this does not seem to occur.

After you have fetched your child from a period of 'time-out', do not demand apologies or engage in recriminations. Be friendly and matter-of-fact.

In situations where 'time-out' cannot be used, another method of managing aggressive behaviour is to firmly hold a child's arms at her sides for a count of fifteen. She is then released. If the behaviour recurs, this should be repeated. This method is known as 'brief restraint'.

While holding the child, you should not interact with her. The idea is to stop the pleasure of walking and running about for a few moments, not to make the restraint itself a form of positive interaction.

There are some situations where a child becomes used to being rewarded for unwanted behaviour. An example of this is when prolonged crying in the cot eventually results in the desired parent's reappearance. The withdrawal of such a reward is called 'extinction'.

There are two ways of doing this: abrupt withdrawal or gradual withdrawal. The latter is sometimes referred to as 'controlled crying', and is usually favoured. In this method, you will need to wait longer and longer periods before returning to your child. The attention given to the child on your return should be minimal.

Be prepared for the behaviour to worsen initially. This usually lasts a few days, and, if you hold firm, the behaviour will rapidly diminish and disappear. After a variable period (a week or two), there is often a reappearance of the behaviour, as if your child is testing whether the new rules still apply. If you continue to be consistent, the behaviour will cease.

Before embarking on an extinction programme, both parents should prepare themselves for a trying time. During the period when the behaviour worsens, it is important to support one another.

BEFORE YOU ATTEMPT BEHAVIOUR MODIFICATION

Behaviour modification is straightforward in theory—encourage and reward good behaviour, discourage bad. In practice, it can be very difficult. The following should be taken into consideration:

● **Consider your child's developmental level**

Assess your child's behaviour and decide whether it is appropriate for the stage of development she has reached. Disregard her chronological age, and think of her developmental age. If you do not know the age at which your child is functioning developmentally, you should seek the opinion of a psychologist, so that this can be assessed. If the behaviour that your child is demonstrating is appropriate for her developmental age, it may help you understand why she is behaving in this way. You may choose to wait until she outgrows this stage, or set more modest goals.

You also need to keep your child's developmental level in

mind in the way in which you reward her good behaviour. One cannot expect a four-year-old child whose understanding is at an eighteen-month level to be able to co-operate with a star-chart or a delayed reward system. A child at this level must be given a tangible reward at the time she behaves in the desired manner.

● Try to be as consistent as possible

Decide on the limits you are going to set on what your child may and may not do, and then try to stick to them. Complete consistency is, of course, impossible, but aim for as much consistency as possible. You should not be discouraged if others do not set the same limits as you do. Children can accept different limits from different people. What confuses them is when one person acts inconsistently.

● A practical change may be all that is needed

If your child has an unwanted behaviour, always ask yourself if some practical change would make it easier to manage. This may be easier than embarking on a behaviour management programme.

If a child with Down syndrome continually enters an older sibling's room and untidies it or damages possessions, the easiest way to resolve the problem may be by putting a bolt on the door that can be closed by the sibling but cannot be reached by the child. The problem of a child who takes chocolate bars from the grocery cupboard may be solved by child-proof locks or simply by hiding the chocolates. Being close to the problem and under stress, parents often find it difficult to stand back and think of a practical solution.

● Tackle one behaviour at a time

If your child demonstrates a number of unwanted behaviours, you will need to decide which you want to tackle first. Some-times the choice is easy—the most worrying might be the most amenable to change. Behaviours are sometimes related, and eradicating one may get rid of others. If you are feeling over-whelmed by a number of behaviour problems, it may be more rewarding to tackle a relatively minor problem first.

- **Do not ignore your own stress**

  Children and their behaviour can be extremely stressful to parents. They do not obey reasonable rules, and the behaviour of a difficult child can create tremendous stress in a family and drive parents apart. Both of you need a chance to express your feelings about the child. There are times when you need to get away and have a break. It may be a matter of having your child minded while you go for a walk, listening to some music, or soaking in a warm bath. Regular respite-care is probably the most effective way of ensuring that everyone has a break. It has the additional advantage that some behaviour management techniques may be carried out by the staff at the respite-care cottage.

- **You may need help**

  It is often difficult for parents to plan and implement behaviour management programmes on their own. If, after trying the methods described above, you have not succeeded, do not hesitate to consult a psychologist or programme officer (some doctors are skilled in this area). This can usually be arranged through your community mental handicap team or child development centre. The psychologist will spend time finding out about the behaviour, and also about the home situation. A visit to your home to talk to you is often needed. He or she will then ask you to record your observations, so that the pattern of the behaviour can be analysed, as well as the factors influencing it. This will also allow you to monitor whether the behaviour modification programme is succeeding. The psychologist will then plan, with your help, what you will need to do to modify the behaviour. He or she will keep in contact and advise you along the way.

  Schools can also help you with some programmes, and may even take over the major share of teaching behaviour such as toilet training or good eating habits, which you can then follow through at home.

MANAGING SOME SPECIFIC BEHAVIOURS

Here is some advice on managing behaviours which often crop up. Advice on managing these behaviours should be read in conjunction with the principles of behaviour management already outlined in this chapter.

Tongue-protruding

Children with Down syndrome often have a habit of protruding (sticking out) their tongues. This is due to the combination of a larger than average tongue and a smaller than average mouth.

During early infancy, many babies put out their tongues at times, and this can be ignored. But from one year onwards, it is necessary to start teaching your child to keep her tongue in her mouth. You do not want to make too much fuss about this, or you will encourage rather than discourage the behaviour. Sometimes, it is enough to give your child a verbal cue, such as 'tongue in', or later just 'in' in the same tone. You may also need to give her a gentle tap under the chin, or touch her lower lip by brushing it upwards gently with the side of your finger. At the same time, you should say 'no'. Praise her for putting it back in. If you do this fairly consistently, she may stop protruding her tongue.

Dribbling

Children with Down syndrome, because of their low tone, are more likely to keep their mouths open and dribble during early childhood. If the child is reminded to swallow, this habit usually stops. It may also be necessary to close the child's mouth gently as described above. With these measures, most children stop dribbling by the time they are about four years of age.

In the rare case where dribbling persists beyond this age, it may be necessary to consider an operation to decrease saliva production. Appropriate operations include cutting the nerve to one of the salivary glands and removing the gland on the other side, or re-routing the ducts of two of the salivary glands so that they open at the back of the mouth, and the saliva runs straight down the throat. These operations are usually performed by an ear, nose, and throat surgeon, and are generally successful.

Overactivity (hyperactivity)

It is normal for children at a fifteen-month to a three-year-old developmental level to be distractable, impulsive, impersistent with tasks, and continually restless and on the go. The basic difficulty for these children is in channelling their attention into one activity for any period of time. As they get. older, this behaviour settles down.

The way you can help your child is to set appropriate goals for her, such as expecting her to remain at the table during mealtimes for at least five minutes, and then gradually increasing your expectations. Be generous with your praise when goals are achieved.

Give her an opportunity to burn off extra energy with active play. A trampoline is good in this respect (if her neck X-ray is clear). Swimming is also a good way to get rid of pent-up energy. Allow her to go out, even if it is raining. Rain will not harm her, but staying indoors for protracted periods can be very trying for all concerned.

If possible, avoid restrictive, confusing, and over-stimulating places if your child seems to be adversely affected by these.

Children who are hyperactive often have little sense of time sequence. A fixed routine may have a settling effect on such children. For example, at bed time, the routine may be that the child has her evening meal, followed by her bath, and a bed-time story. A fairly regular course of events enables the child to anticipate the next activity, and helps to keep her calm and easier to manage. Set routines particularly help children who may have difficulty understanding verbal explanations of what is going to happen next, but who quickly become used to a routine if they are actually involved in it.

If your child has poor attending skills, make certain that you have her attention when you give her an instruction. It may be necessary to touch her gently and make certain that she is looking at you.

A diet and medicines sometimes used in the management of overactive children are discussed in Chapter 15.

The child who wanders off when out

Children who abscond are a terrible worry to parents. Firstly, you should make sure that the child has a bracelet with her name, address, and telephone number, in case she ever goes missing. If possible, do not take her with you when you go to places that are very crowded, or where you have a lot of other responsibilities in addition to the child. Using a little harness with reins is something that parents often feel unhappy about, but it is quite comfortable for the child, and preferable to having her run into the road. When the child does stay with you when out walking, reward her. Do not expect the child to keep up with you if you are walking very fast. It is difficult for young children with Down syndrome to remain at an adult's side, and they are often better off in a push-chair.

Tantrums

Tantrums are seen both in normal toddlers and in children with Down syndrome of that developmental age. Tantrums usually come on if the child is frustrated or thwarted.

When a tantrum begins, it is best to acknowledge the child's frustration. Although the child may not react, your verbalization of her desire immediately makes her aware that you understand how she feels. Then try divert her attention to another activity. If this does not work, pretend to ignore the tantrum. Any further attention will only increase the behaviour. Keep ignoring the tantrum until you feel yourself becoming exasperated, at which point you should use the 'time-out' technique. Fetch your child only when both of you are calm again. There should be no recriminations, and you should interact with her as if nothing has happened. Tantrums usually diminish as the child gets older, particularly as her communication skills improve.

Hitting and biting other children

This behaviour often starts as an attempt by a child with poor language skills to communicate with others in some way. Children under a developmental age of four usually do not have the ability to empathize with others, and are often quite surprised by the negative reaction which their behaviour causes.

It is best to use the 'time-out' or the 'brief restraint' technique described earlier in this chapter. Children usually do not persist with this behaviour, for the simple reason that they start meeting up with children who do not tolerate it and retaliate. From her peers, the child often learns the lesson which her parents were unable to teach her.

Destructive behaviour

Occasionally, a child may be destructive towards toys and other objects. Firstly, try to keep delicate things out of her reach. It may be better to put fragile ornaments high up, rather than trying to teach her not to touch them. Choose robust toys. Children may become destructive when given toys which are too complicated, and therefore frustrating.

Try not to show too much reaction to the destruction of objects when this occurs, as it may only reinforce destructive behaviour. Try to redirect her attention to more constructive play or, if that is not possible, divert her energy to physical play outside. If this fails, practise 'time-out'.

When you go out visiting, always take some of your child's favourite toys with you, or keep some special toy for this purpose. Whenever possible, try to avoid places where destructive behaviour would be a particular problem. Parents are usually anxious when taking out a child who can be destructive. When out, make certain that your anxiety does not make you excessively strict with your child, as this may make her even more tense and destructive.

9. A guide to services

As the parent of a child with Down syndrome, you will have special needs over and above those of most other parents. It is important to know how to get the most out of services available to your child.

Services are continually changing, and it is difficult to keep track of them. You have to keep your eyes open, read advertisements, and talk to other parents. The latter can be particularly helpful with first-hand experience of services they have used. Some local authorities produce excellent guides to services available in their areas. The description in a leaflet or an advertisement is often incomplete, however, and it is useful to talk to a professional who has knowledge of local services, and can give you the benefit of his or her experience.

This chapter deals mainly with services for children with Down syndrome. Services exclusively for adults are discussed in Chapter 14.

YOUR CHILD'S KEY WORKER

Parents of children with Down syndrome need information about appropriate local services for their child. They also need periodic support and advice about ways of helping their child. Most parents find it very helpful to have one experienced professional who has the time and the expertise to give them this sort of information, advice, and support.

Although your family doctor or general paediatrician would be the best person to co-ordinate the medical care of your child, doctors often do not have the time to acquire a detailed knowledge of services for children with intellectual disability. They also may not have the time to talk to parents about these at length. For this reason, it is often better to have a non-medical professional to take on this role. This worker should be easy to contact, approachable, and able to work with the other professionals who are involved with your child's care.

Such a worker is often referred to as the child's 'care co-ordinator' or 'key worker'. A key worker acts as a 'broker', negotiating for services on the parents' behalf. He or she will usually be prepared to accompany parents on visits to clinics, doctors, and schools if they wish.

In the United Kingdom and Australia, there are government-funded community-based teams*, where a member of the team takes on the role of key worker. In other countries, if a similar team does not exist, parents should request that their nearest child development centre provides such a worker.

THE CHILD DEVELOPMENT CENTRE

It is a good idea to arrange a visit to a child development centre sometime during the first six months of your child's life. These centres will provide a comprehensive assessment of a child's abilities and needs. The assessment process is described in the next chapter.

EARLY INTERVENTION SERVICES

Early intervention services, or therapy centres as they are sometimes called, are usually staffed by occupational therapists, physiotherapists, speech therapists, and special educators. The role of these professionals, and the early intervention service they provide, are discussed in more detail in Chapter 11.

HOME HELP SERVICES

Home help services provide support for families who experience difficulty in maintaining their home or family because of their child's disability. There is often a nominal fee for this service.

The staff will help with cleaning the home, cooking, shopping, laundry, and other domestic tasks. They may take the child to intervention, and carry out some of the programme at home. In some cases, they may help by simply taking the child

---

* UK: Community Mental Handicap Team or District Handicap Team. Australia: Community Services for the Developmentally Disabled (NSW), Office of Intellectual Disability (Victoria).

out for a walk or to the park, in order to give the parents a break.

If you need this sort of help, due to the extra load imposed by your child's condition, you should find out whether such a service exists in your area.

DOWN SYNDROME ASSOCIATIONS

In most English-speaking countries there are associations formed by parents of children with Down syndrome (see Appendix). Such associations vary in their activities. They generally produce a regular newsletter, have meetings where parents can share experiences, run a library with books containing information of interest to parents, and sometimes provide special information leaflets and kits. Some have become very well organized, and produce audio-visual information on Down syndrome, run conferences, and even sponsor research. There is usually an annual membership fee.

RESPITE-CARE SERVICES

Children need an opportunity to stay away from home with other children of a similar age in order to gain more independence, have fun, and give the rest of the family a break. Many children visit cousins or friends to achieve this, but some children do not have this opportunity. For this reason, there are services that provide temporary respite-care for children with intellectual disability.

Many parents find it difficult to use respite-care services, feeling that they should shoulder all the responsibility for their child's care. Parents may defer using respite-care, claiming that they will use it when they need it. Unfortunately, this often means that the pressures of looking after the child build up, and a crisis occurs, so that respite-care has to be used. The child then faces a bigger adjustment, suddenly finding himself away from home for the first time.

Respite-care provides children with Down syndrome with important training in independent living. In addition, having a break from one another is good for both the child and the family. When the child gets home, the quality of the time that parent and child spend together more than compensates for the period of separation.

Respite-care may be provided by a host family or individual, or at a respite-care cottage.

Host families

There are some agencies which arrange for volunteers to care for children with a disability.

If the parents of a child with Down syndrome are happy with the arrangement, the child will spend a short time with the host family or individual. If the stay is successful, a series of visits may be arranged. These visits may vary from a few hours to days or weeks. The agency which arranges the service will usually charge a nominal fee, and the host family are paid an amount which covers expenses.

This sort of service not only helps parents, but also provides an opportunity for the host family or individual to enjoy looking after the child, and for children within the host family to gain a better understanding of disability. Many such relationships endure for a long time.

Some parents have difficulty finding a suitable host family or individual. Others do not feel happy about non-professionals looking after their child. You need to make up your own mind whether this sort of service would suit you.

Respite-care cottages

There are now more and more cottages being established to provide respite-care for children with intellectual disability. These cottages often have six or seven places for children. Bookings usually need to be made in advance, but one or two places are often kept for emergencies. Children are looked after by professionals with training in the care of disabled children, and a busy programme with outings and other activities is arranged. Most children enjoy going to such cottages, and look forward to their visits.

When your child first starts having respite-care, you should leave him for short periods of time to get used gradually to the new environment and the staff. Once your child enjoys staying at a respite-care cottage, you should try to arrange a regular booking, so that he accepts this as part of his routine, and you have a chance to make plans in advance.

RECREATIONAL SERVICES

By involving your child in some leisure activity, you not only improve his health and occupy his time, but help him learn to enjoy himself and to get on with others. These skills will be of benefit to him in the years ahead.

First of all, look at your child's abilities and preferences, and find out what is available in your area. A *recreational officer* or *worker from the mental handicap team* may be able to give you some suggestions. You may also be able to obtain a *recreational newsletter*, which tells you about local activities.

Many parents feel strongly that their child should take part in normal leisure activities. This is satisfactory if appropriate activities can be found; but it is a pity to prevent your child from taking part in special activities for children with disabilities if he would benefit from these.

When your child plays with other children, you may need to give him some direction. Playing with friends is often most successful if organized around some activity, such as a visit to the park or the swimming pool, so that the children do not become aimless and bored.

There are now some *'leisure buddy schemes'*, where normal volunteers link up with a disabled person and integrate him into a particular recreational activity. This is rewarding for both the child and the volunteer. It may be something as simple as taking the child to the park and playing with him, or including him in a Scout group or soccer team.

Children with Down syndrome can often take part in *sporting activities for normal children*, provided that the organizers are willing to make the necessary modifications. For example, the child with Down syndrome may be able to play softball with a larger bat. He may take the role of score-keeper or equipment supervisor. Make sure that such tasks improve your child's self-esteem and do not diminish it.

Many children enjoy taking part in activities with other children of the same ability. There are now many *leisure activities for the disabled*, and of these, swimming, horse-riding, dancing, drama, ten-pin bowling, and scouting seem to be particularly popular with children with Down syndrome. Find out whether any of these activities take place in your area. In addition, enterprising parents can sometimes get together and arrange a weekly activity, such as an aerobics class for a group of disabled children.

Hobbies give children a chance to occupy themselves, and also to meet other people. Hobbies such as weaving or collecting stamps are also an opportunity to improve a child's self-esteem. Gardening is a satisfying activity, and, if you have a garden, try to allocate a portion for your child to cultivate under your supervision.

AFTER-SCHOOL AND SCHOOL HOLIDAY CARE

In some areas, after-school care is available for children with disabilities. In some cases, the siblings of children with Down syndrome are also able to attend such after-school care sessions. Most programmes keep children busy with interesting and enjoyable activities, and this is a very helpful service for working parents and those in need of some time to themselves in the afternoon.

Holiday camps for children with Down syndrome and other causes of intellectual disability are often run on a regular basis. Most children with Down syndrome thoroughly enjoy this activity, and benefit from the opportunity to have fun, meet with other children, and gain more independence. There are also other school holiday programmes run on a daily basis, which help to keep children entertained and active when school has broken up.

You can usually find out about these programmes from your local special school or mental handicap team.

FINANCIAL ASSISTANCE

All children place a financial burden upon their parents. Children with Down syndrome, because of their special needs for therapy, toys, medical procedures, and additional care, impose a greater financial burden. This is recognized in most countries, and special allowances are usually available.

In applying for benefits, do not understate your child's needs for care and supervision. Make certain that the clerk who evaluates your application gains a clear understanding of the financial and emotional burdens that you bear.

If you do not find out about a benefit until some time after you are entitled to it, or if there is a delay before you are able to apply, find out if it is possible to backdate the claim. A letter from a professional who knows your child may be useful.

Sometimes, even straightforward claims for benefits can be unexpectedly refused. In this situation, you should exercise your right to appeal. You may need to obtain the advice of your child's key worker or a social worker.

LEGAL ASSISTANCE

You should draw up a will to provide for your child with Down syndrome as early as possible. Without a will, you cannot be certain that your child will be provided for in the best possible way after your death.

As your child with Down syndrome is unlikely to be able to look after your estate on his own, the setting up of a trust is advisable. In drawing up a will, selecting trustees, and other legal issues relating to your child, it is important to seek the advice of a lawyer with special expertise in the area of the legal rights of people with intellectual disability. Your local assessment centre or mental handicap team should be able to direct you to an appropriate lawyer or legal agency.

10. Assessment

Every child with Down syndrome has individual strengths and weaknesses. No single intervention or educational plan will be suitable for all. It is therefore necessary for each child's unique needs to be appraised in a regular and thorough way.

WHAT IS AN ASSESSMENT?

An assessment is a process whereby a professional or group of professionals evaluate a child's abilities at a particular time, and make recommendations based on her needs. The needs that are most often focused upon are for appropriate intervention during the pre-school years, and appropriate school placement as the child gets closer to school age. A complete assessment will also include looking at the child's health needs, and at ways of helping the child and the family benefit as much as possible from services that are available. For you, the parents, it is also a chance to sit back and review your child's progress away from the hustle and bustle of day-to-day activities.

ASSESSMENTS SHOULD BE REGULAR

'Assessment' is a word that often makes parents feel anxious. They are concerned that important decisions about their child's future may be based on her performance on a particular day. Any good assessment will, however, take into account the parents', therapists', and teachers' reports about a child's skills and behaviour demonstrated in the past. There should be adequate time for the child to relax on the day, and you should always observe your child's assessment, and be able to comment on whether she has performed up to her usual standard or not.

The best way to avoid inappropriate decisions is for assessments to become a regular part of your child's programme from early childhood. This allows serial evaluation of her progress, and provides a more accurate picture of your child's development.

WHERE TO GO FOR AN ASSESSMENT

Assessments are now a legal right for children with disabilities in the UK and USA. Even where this is not the case, it is usually easy to arrange an assessment in countries such as Australia, Canada, New Zealand, the Republic of Ireland, and South Africa. There are three ways in which an assessment can be arranged.

1. Education Department

In England and Wales, the 1981 Education Act allows parents to request a free assessment for their child under the age of two years, and lays a duty on the education authority to provide assessment of children after this age.

In the USA, a free evaluation prior to the drawing up of an individualized education plan is one of the key provisions of Public Law 94–142. The evaluation must be provided by the age of three, but some states have lowered this to the new-born period.

In England and the USA, parental involvement in the assessment is ensured by legislation. In these countries, the Education Department also has to seek medical advice about the child, usually from your own doctor.

In other countries, Education Departments usually have psychologists who will assess children with special needs prior to school entry, but usually not at an earlier age. Assessments by Department of Education psychologists vary, and, in some cases, other professionals involved in the child's care may not be consulted. The options mentioned below may therefore be preferable.

2. Child development centres

Child development centres now exist in children's hospitals in most parts of the world. They are staffed by paediatricians, psychologists, social workers, and sometimes nurses, therapists, and teachers. They provide a 'one-stop' assessment of your child's abilities by a number of professionals from different disciplines, working as a team. They usually have close links with education authorities, and their findings are invariably accepted without the need to duplicate tests. The multidisciplinary staff has extensive knowledge and experience of children with Down syndrome and other conditions associated with disability.

Many parents prefer to have their child assessed at a child development centre, even where Education Department assessments are available. They prefer the convenience of seeing all the professionals at one time. This approach also allows more open communication for all concerned.

Perhaps the greatest advantage is that this type of assessment is not confined to educational issues alone. A wide range of problems experienced by parents can be discussed. Members of the assessment team are able to provide information about local services. They can advise about both government and private schools, as well as other services such as respite-care, pre-school groups and classes, vacation programmes, and welfare benefits.

To arrange an assessment at a child development centre, phone the children's hospital nearest to you. In some areas of the UK, district handicap teams provide a similar assessment to that available at a child development centre.

3. Psychologists in private practice

There are educational psychologists in private practice who will test your child, for a fee, and report their findings to you. These can then be combined with reports from your own doctor and other professionals such as therapists, to be forwarded to the Education Department if necessary.

WHO PERFORMS THE ASSESSMENT?

The best assessment is one performed by professionals from a number of different disciplines. Professionals most commonly involved are a psychologist, a paediatrician, and a social worker.

A *psychologist* is trained to assess your child's intellectual strengths and weaknesses, and evaluate her educational needs.

He or she will also have training and experience in managing behaviour, and can give helpful advice if there are any concerns in this regard.

A *paediatrician* will be able to detect the presence of any physical impairments, and their bearing upon your child's education. He or she will arrange special medical testing, if needed, and answer your questions about further pregnancies and other health issues.

The involvement of a *social worker* complements the role of the psychologist and paediatrician by ensuring that your child's educational needs are seen within the context of her family. He or she will ensure that issues, such as transport to and from school, after-school care, and other appropriate services are addressed. Most importantly, he or she will guide you through the procedure of assessment and school selection, so that you are kept informed and are consulted throughout. A social worker will accompany you on visits to schools and other facilities if you wish, and will help you appeal against any educational placement decisions with which you disagree.

Some centres also have physiotherapists, occupational therapists, and speech therapists; however, since the major contribution of these therapists is in providing therapy, their roles will be discussed in the next chapter.

WHEN SHOULD ASSESSMENTS BE PERFORMED?

Assessments should begin when your child is about four months of age and continue at six- to twelve-monthly intervals until she enters school. No reliable prediction of your child's future abilities can be made until she is about three or four years of age. When younger, however, her development and needs at the time of assessment can be discussed, and you can be given advice about helping her. You will be able to find out about appropriate services, and, in addition, you have an opportunity to discuss those things that concern you. Early assessments also allow you to get to know the assessment team, so that later assessments are more relaxed.

Once your child starts school, reviews may be timed in accordance with your needs and the legal requirements of your country. In the United Kingdom, the Education Act stipulates that the Education Authority should review your child annually and reassess her between $12\frac{1}{2}$ and $14\frac{1}{2}$ years. In the USA, PL94–142 ensures annual reviews until 21 years (18 years in some states). In other countries, you should ensure that a re-assessment is performed when your child is about 10–12 years, so that issues related to puberty can be discussed. Another re-assessment at about 14–15 years allows for vocational guidance.

DEVELOPMENTAL AND INTELLIGENCE TESTS

When a child's skills are below that of an average two- or three-year-old, developmental tests are used to assess her abilities. These tests evaluate the child's progress in all areas of development (see Chapter 5). Once the child is more capable, intelligence tests can be used. These are primarily concerned with the measurement of intelligence, both that which is related to language ability and that which requires manipulation of objects.

Tests of development and intelligence have come in for criticism over the last few years; however, they still form an important part of establishing a child's abilities and needs. They must be performed by an experienced psychologist, and interpreted with care. The results of such tests should be regarded as only part of the child's assessment, and need to be interpreted in the light of reports of the child's development, observation of her play, and the results of any previous tests.

It is very important to watch your child being tested. This demystifies the process, and helps you understand how the tester came to his or her conclusions. It also enables you to inform the tester if your child's performance was not up to her usual standard.

In order to observe testing, you can either stay with your child or watch through a one-way screen if there is one available. It is better to remain with a younger child. Try not to become involved in the testing; but smile at the child in an encouraging way if she turns to look at you. Once your child is older, the presence of a parent in the room may act as a distraction, and it is often best for you to watch through a one-way screen.

The tests that are generally used have been administered to many hundreds of children to obtain standards for different ages. Tasks are presented in a specific order, with the easier ones first. They then become progressively more advanced, to establish at what level they become too difficult for the child. Every child who does the test will be presented with tasks that are easy, as well as tasks that are too difficult for her. This is necessary in order to find out the exact level at which the child is functioning.

During the course of the test, a picture of the child's developmental progress can be formed, both for specific areas of development and for her development as a whole. Sometimes, a great deal of information can be gained from the way a child tackles tasks, even if she is unable to succeed.

One of the frustrating things for parents watching their child being tested, is that the way in which the tester asks questions and presents the puzzles and other materials cannot be varied. As standards for children of different ages were developed by administering the tests in a particular way, the test must be carried out in the same way if these standards are to remain valid. Parents often feel that their child would have been able to succeed at a task, had the tester worded the question differently or given some extra assistance. While the tester should be interested in these observations by the parent, only responses to the standard way of testing can be scored. Much of the intelligence needed for everyday life requires an ability to perform tasks that may be presented differently from the way in which the child is accustomed to meet them. Intelligence involves flexibility, as well as ability.

The materials used in most tests are attractive, and children usually enjoy 'playing' with the tester. Occasionally, children are uncooperative, which need not be of concern. Much information can be gained from observing what your child does in free play, asking what she does at home, and from reading the reports of therapists and teachers. If this information is inadequate, retesting or observation of the child at school or home may be necessary.

Do not hesitate to ask questions at the end of the assessment. You should also request that a copy of the report be sent to you.*

---

* It is a good idea to start a file in which all copies of reports pertaining to your child (therapy, school, doctors, assessment, etc.) can be kept in chronological order. Such a file may be useful for professionals who see your child in the future.

It is well known that parents have difficulty remembering everything that they are told at an assessment, and often forget to ask questions. Do not hesitate to phone later with questions that occur to you.

Developmental (or mental) age

The results of a developmental or intelligence test should always be explained to you a short while after the test has been completed. The psychologist usually needs about fifteen minutes to calculate the result.

Psychologists usually explain the results by describing the child's strengths and weaknesses, and pointing out how the child has progressed since she was last tested. The person who does the test may refer to the child as having a particular 'developmental age' (DA) or 'mental age' (MA). This means that her developmental level is more or less like that of a child of that particular age.

You should not attach too much importance to the precise developmental age. It is only a guide to your child's understanding and knowledge of her world and the maturity of her reasoning. It gives you an idea of the behaviour and skills that you can expect from her at that stage in her development. Knowing a child's developmental age assists in knowing how best to respond to her, and in choosing appropriate toys, books, and activities.

Intelligence quotients

Intelligence tests, in addition to determining mental age, also give a score known as an intelligence quotient (IQ). Although this is a useful concept, psychologists are often reluctant to reveal the exact IQ to the parents, because this quotient is so often misunderstood. Although an IQ is expressed as a number, it is not the precise value that is important. In fact, if the IQ could be measured the very next day (a different test would have to be used to make it fair), the precise value would probably be slightly different. What is most important is the range in which the child's IQ score falls.

IQ ranges

It is useful to use terms such as mild, moderate, and severe to describe a range of similar IQ scores. Each range can be

thought of as a broad band or channel (Fig. 18). Most children
with Down syndrome continue to develop within the same IQ
range throughout their lives. Children do move slightly up and
down within a range; but this is of no significance. Children
with scores close to the border between two adjacent ranges
may easily cross over from one to another, and this is also of
no significance. The decision about exactly where one range
begins and another ends is largely arbitrary. Although some
people define the exact limits with great numerical precision,
there is disagreement amongst different authorities. When one
is measuring something that shows slight variation all the time,
it is inappropriate to try to be too accurate about the borders of
its ranges. Nevertheless, it is sometimes useful to think in terms
of a range when trying to plan ahead for a child, provided that
this is not the only aspect taken into account. This limitation
applies to children, but is even more pertinent to adults. In the
latter, IQ ranges are not as useful as looking at how the person
functions in the community, something which is only partially
related to her IQ. Temperament, opportunity, and experience
are equally important.

Terms used for IQ ranges

People with IQs ranging from about 80 to 130 are considered
to have normal intelligence.

An IQ of about 70 to 80 is regarded as demonstrating a
borderline degree of intellectual impairment. Such people
usually manage in the normal stream, but have developed at
between approximately two-thirds to four-fifths of the average
rate of development.

Children and adults with an IQ score below about 70 are
regarded as having an intellectual disability. Other synonymous
terms are 'intellectual handicap', 'mental handicap', and 'mental
retardation'. 'Mental handicap' is the term most frequently used
in the UK, while 'mental retardation' is used widely in the USA.
'Developmental disability' is a broader term, which includes
those with intellectual disability as well as other disabilities.

Most people have a preconception of what intellectual disability means. This is frequently based on someone they knew,
often as a child. It is important to realize that the term covers
children and adults with a wide range of ability; some who are

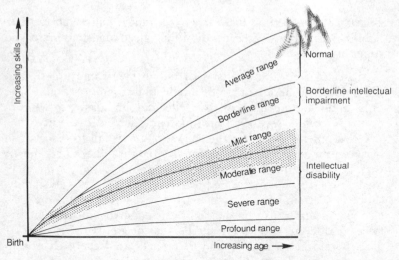

Fig. 18. IQ ranges. Shaded area shows how most, but not all, children and adults with the syndrome develop.

able to live an ordinary life with hardly any special help, and others who need a great deal of care and supervision. It is, therefore, useful to describe intellectual disability according to its severity.

The following terms are usually used. In each case, the eventual adult level of competence is described.

Mild intellectual disability (IQ range from about 50 to 70). Adults with this degree of disability can usually live independently with little supervision.

Moderate intellectual disability (IQ range from about 35 to 50). Adults with this degree of disability will need help with managing their financial affairs, and usually also require some supervision of day-to-day activities such as shopping, cooking, and commuting.

Severe intellectual disability (IQ range from about 20 to 35). Adults with this degree of disability always need a great deal of supervision, although this need not be constant, as many are able to care for themselves in matters such as dressing, eating, washing, and toileting.

Profound intellectual disability (IQ range below about 20). Adults with this degree of disability need constant care and supervision.

Most children and adults with Down syndrome function in the mild or moderate range of intellectual disability. Some have only a borderline degree of intellectual impairment, while a minority have a severe or profound intellectual disability.

Government and other agencies sometimes fail to distinguish between moderate and severe intellectual disability. This means that if your child has a moderate disability, he or she may qualify for services described as being for the 'severely handicapped'. Certain books, particularly those published in the UK, also use a classification that fails to make the distinction between moderate and severe intellectual disability. It is important, therefore, to realize that references to 'severe' handicap may also include 'moderate' disability.

11. Early intervention and pre-school groups

The last two decades have seen increased interest focused on the development of infants and children during the pre-school years. Far greater emphasis is now placed on educational activities during early childhood. Educators have become more involved with the pre-school child, and many pre-school centres have shifted their emphasis from child care to child education.

Educators, physiotherapists, occupational therapists, and speech therapists have also turned their attention to the intellectually disabled pre-school child. The young child with Down syndrome has been particularly singled out for special help because, unlike most children with intellectual disability, his condition is usually diagnosed at birth. Teaching can therefore begin early; and parents will generally find professionals eager to give them advice about stimulating their child.

Such advice, if sensible and realistic, can be a great boon, putting you on the right track and supporting you in raising your child. Unrealistic and impractical advice, on the other hand, places an unnecessary burden on the whole family, and creates false expectations, making you vulnerable to later disappointment.

This chapter describes ways in which you can give your child the best possible chance during the pre-school years, and contains advice on how to avoid being overwhelmed by early childhood intervention.

WHAT IS 'EARLY INTERVENTION'?

The term 'intervention' is used to cover physiotherapy, occupational therapy, speech therapy, and special educational help. Playgroup and pre-school experience is also regarded as a form of intervention. 'Intervention' has replaced the terms 'therapy' and 'treatment' in order to avoid medical connotations, and to emphasize that it is a help rather than a cure. *Early* intervention is intervention given during the period shortly after birth until school starts (at about five years).

DOES IT WORK?

To assess whether early intervention works, we must look at two aspects; the effect on the child, and the effect on the parents:

Effect on the child's development

There have been numerous research studies that attempt to evaluate the effect of intervention on the development of children with Down syndrome. These generally show that children with Down syndrome who received early intervention, functioned better than those who did not receive intervention. On average, those who received intervention scored approximately twenty per cent higher on intelligence testing performed at the time they entered school. This is most heartening, because, as mentioned in the previous chapter, intelligence tests assess those things children have learned for themselves, and not just the things they have been taught.

But it should be noted that the twenty per cent difference is based on the *average* scores for two groups of children. We have no way of knowing what the impact of intervention is on an individual child. Presumably some children would show a greater change than this average, while others would show little or no change.

To keep the benefit of intervention in perspective, it is worth looking at studies that compare children with Down syndrome raised in institutions with those raised at home. These studies have consistently shown that children raised at home score, on average, fifty per cent higher on tests of intelligence in the early school years. At one time this was thought to reflect the fact that it was often the more severely disabled children who were placed in institutions. But similar results have been obtained for children with Down syndrome placed in institutions at birth, when it would have been too early to predict their degree of disability. This research would suggest that bringing up children with Down syndrome at home has been the most important factor in their improved competence. At home, parents help their child by doing what comes naturally to them: talking to him, listening and responding to him, including him in activities, widening his experiences, reading to him, and helping him to have contact with other adults and children. In other words, by normal parenting.

In the light of these findings, early intervention should be viewed as a worth while, but not indispensable, adjunct to the more important learning experience that you give your child through normal parenting.

Very little work has been done to assess whether the benefits derived from early intervention continue beyond the pre-school years. A few studies have suggested that some of the benefits are lost by the time the child reaches eight years of age. If this is true, it may represent a failure of the school system to maintain the gains, rather than any short-comings of the intervention programme.

Effect on the parents

Parents have generally been enthusiastic in their response to early intervention programmes. They feel the programme gives them a more positive attitude towards their child and his development, and helps them respond to him in a way that is appropriate to his level of development. It means that there is someone to listen to them and assist them with the challenges of raising a child with Down syndrome. It also allows them to meet other parents, share experiences, and gain support. As one mother said,

The doctor was so negative. He only spoke about what Michael wouldn't be able to do. Therapy gave us new hope. We were so surprised by how he improved. Without the programme I would not have known where to begin. It has been a lot of hard work, but it has been well worth it. I feel that the therapists have helped me to teach Michael practically everything he knows.

There is little doubt that a good intervention programme can be of great benefit; however, intervention does not suit all parents. Some parents find that the intervention sessions and the programme make excessive demands on their time, and they do not feel natural or happy with the things they are expected to do. They may find that, for them, slow gains become more apparent when closely monitored by the intervention programme, and make them feel less happy about their child's progress. These parents can be reassured by knowing that many children with Down syndrome who received no structured early intervention have made good progress. Some parents do very well on their own, without the guidance of an intervention programme, and it is not essential for all.

WHAT DIFFERENT THERAPISTS DO

Early Intervention Services or Therapy Services usually consist of a team made up of an occupational therapist, a physiotherapist, a speech therapist, and a special educator. Some speech therapists prefer to be called speech pathologists.

The physiotherapist

The physiotherapist is usually the first person you will meet in an intervention team. He or she is involved with posture and movement. The fact that gross motor development is the most prominent aspect of development during the first two years of life means that the physiotherapist tends to be the person who provides most of the help during this period. But this form of intervention should be very low-keyed at this stage. Tone will improve of its own accord, and the main role of the physiotherapist is to help find ways of encouraging the child to make appropriate movements, by attention to the child's posture and environment, rather than by exercise or manipulation of the child's body. The physiotherapist will also show you how to hold your child and how to position him so that he is in the best situation to use his hands and eyes in order to learn more about his environment. The role of the physiotherapist diminishes once the child is walking.

The occupational therapist

An occupational therapist can play a role in helping you to teach eye and hand co-ordination skills and some early academic skills. In the early years, he or she will recommend appropriate toys and play activities for your child. An occupational therapist can often find ways of breaking up a complex task, such as dressing, into separate steps, so that it is easier for a child to learn.

The speech therapist

The speech therapist is involved in teaching communication. He or she will assess your child's understanding and use of language, as well as his clarity of speech. Some speech therapists also have special expertise in other movements involving the mouth, and will give advice on discouraging a child from poking out his tongue or dribbling. They will also assist with feeding if difficulties arise.

The special educator

The special educator is a teacher with special training that equips him or her to help children with intellectual disability to learn in academic areas. He or she is concerned with early cognitive abilities, such as matching and sorting shapes and colours. Preliminary academic skills that eventually lead to reading, writing, and number-work are of particular interest to special educators in the pre-school years. Special educators also try to cultivate better attending skills and work habits in children from an early age.

Other workers

In some programmes, the main teacher for the child may be a nurse or health educator. A non-professional who has been trained and is supervised by a therapist or educator may also be able to carry out the programme with the child.

HOW THE TEACHING IS CARRIED OUT

Some intervention programmes adopt a low-keyed approach, with the interventionist seeing the parents every month or so, and giving advice concerning ways of helping the child. At the other end of the scale are programmes in which the child is given one-to-one training by the early intervention staff on a daily basis. There is no evidence to show that more intensive intervention gets better results. Most studies suggest that in the early years, guidance for parents is the most important aspect of intervention.

WHERE DOES IT TAKE PLACE?

Early intervention may be home-based, centre-based, or nursery-school-based. Each form has its own advantages, and some services will provide a mixture of different models.

Home-based intervention may be easier for some parents, as they do not have to travel. It also has the advantage that the child can be observed in his own environment. The interventionist can give advice about incorporating activities into your daily routine, and modifying things at home to best help the child.

Centre-based intervention gives parents a chance to get out of the house and have a change of routine. It also means that they meet other parents with similar problems. There is usually better equipment at a centre, some of which may be borrowed by parents for periods of time (intervention centres often have a toy-library).

HOW TO GET THE MOST OUT OF INTERVENTION

- **Only do things you feel happy about**

  You know your own child and your family's needs better than anyone else. You should try to find a programme that suits your needs, and never agree to institute any intervention that does not feel right for you and your family.

- **Do not overdo it**

  Parents who want to take part in an intervention programme should guard against overdoing it. After the initial shock of finding out that your child has Down syndrome, it is easy to put all your energies into an early intervention programme, and allow yourself to believe, perhaps subconsciously, that you will be able to 'cure' your child. Intervention is a great help, but it is not a cure for Down syndrome.

  Involving your child in more and more intervention will not make him progress faster. In fact, the reverse is often true. If you make excessive demands on him, he will inevitably experience failure, and become unwilling to attempt tasks. In the process of learning, the development of a child's self-esteem is as important as the acquisition of other skills. In addition, if you spend long periods of time taking your child to intervention sessions, as well as doing work with him at home, the rest of the family will eventually suffer.

Do not hesitate to tell your child's therapist if the programme seems excessive. In their enthusiasm, therapists may make too many demands on your time and energy. This is a particular hazard when your child is seen by more than one therapist, and their individual demands accumulate.

Everyone needs to have a break. School years are divided into terms because school-aged children need a period of respite every so often. The pre-schooler with Down syndrome needs at least as many breaks during the year. These should be provided by the intervention programme, so that therapists, parents, and the child have a chance to recover their enthusiasm for the next period of therapy.

If at any time your child is showing signs of becoming resistant to sessions, you should consider taking a break. If you try to persevere in this situation, you run the risk of your child developing unwanted behaviour in an attempt to avoid tasks. He is likely to become negative about therapy for some time. If you stop for a while and start again at a later date with a new approach, you are more likely to succeed.

● **What should he learn?**

Wherever possible, intervention should aim to teach the child practical skills. Intervention should not focus too much on puzzles and building tasks, but should also concentrate on self-help and social tasks such as dressing, sharing with other children, and toilet training.

It is sometimes worth while working on a particular task at which a child wants to succeed. For example, if a four-year-old particularly wants to be able to kick a ball, because this is an activity in which his brothers and sisters engage, a therapist may be able to find ways to help the child master this activity. Some therapists do not like to teach these individual skills, preferring to follow a standard check-list of tasks. But such individual skills are often quickly learned, because the child is very motivated. The therapist can help by breaking down the skill into a number of steps, and finding ways in which these can be practised to achieve success. The whole process can be a very rewarding one for everyone concerned. You should therefore be on the look-out for particular skills which your child wants to learn. Of course, your child must be developmentally ready to learn the skill.

- **Strong and weak areas of development**

  Intervention often concentrates on the child's weaker areas. Most children are aware from an early age of the things they find difficult. Like the rest of us, they tend to want to do the things they are better at. Any intervention programme must, therefore, allow ample opportunity for a child to do those things he is good at, in addition to those he finds difficult. This is important for his self-confidence.

  If, for example, your child is good at kicking a ball, and enjoys this activity, but dislikes doing drawings, which he finds difficult, make certain you spend at least as much time having fun kicking balls as you do practising pencil skills.

  If you spend time with your child practising a task he finds difficult, always end the session with something he finds easy and enjoyable.

- **You are more than a teacher**

  Interventionists often emphasize the fact that you, the parent, should regard yourself as your child's teacher. But you should remember that, while your child may have many teachers, only you can be your child's parent. The relationship between child and parent should not merely become that of teacher and pupil. There must be time for unstructured play, for spontaneity, and for enjoyment for its own sake. One cannot treat every interaction with one's child as an opportunity for learning, without the relationship becoming stilted. Early childhood is so short. Do not let it pass by without enjoying your child.

- **Generalizing skills**

  Children with Down syndrome often have difficulty in generalizing the skills they have learned. This means that a skill learned in a particular situation is often not applied to a new situation. A child may be able to put a square inset into a particular puzzle, but when he is given a new puzzle with a similar inset, he may not be able to do it. This means that there should be a lot of variety in any intervention programme. A child needs to meet different problems, to increase his repertoire of responses so that he can cope with a number of situations.

A task, such as doing puzzles, is often taught by prompting the child with a particular word, such as 'put'. This must be varied, or the child will only perform the task in response to the prompt. This skill may then remain an isolated skill, unapplied in everyday situations.

• **The check-list approach**
Inventories of skills that get ticked off as they are achieved are a help to parents, as they give them some short-term goal to aim for, and a sense of satisfaction if the skill is achieved. But the inventory approach has some disadvantages. The order in which skills are attained in different children varies. Some children bypass some stages.

Do not pay too much attention to the multitude of individual skills on a tick sheet. Try, rather, to take a broader approach, noting the more significant milestones along the way.

• **Homework**
Intervention that is practised at home should always be natural and fit in with the home routine. You are teaching your child even when you may not realize that you are. A lot of teaching can be done by making certain that the child with Down syndrome is not left out of household activities, and that you remember to explain what you are doing. For example, instead of sitting and colour-matching beads or other similar toys, you could, while cutting up vegetables for a salad, get your child to lend a hand by sorting out similarly coloured vegetables.

One-to-one sessions at home should not be prolonged, because children quickly become restless. Your goal should be modest, and appropriate to your child's level of development.

• **Make sure your child is assessed regularly**
When your child is involved in an intervention programme, he should have regular assessments, as described in the previous chapter.

Parents sometimes feel that the therapist or teacher who is seeing their child in the intervention programme is able to do any assessments that are needed. But assessment is a specialized task, different from that of teaching or providing therapy.

Therapists or teachers may use a particular type of assessment, which entails looking at a child's present skills and making plans for the next series of learning tasks. The tests which are used for this sort of assessment are called 'criterion-referenced' tests. For each skill, your child will be compared to an average (normal) child.

But it is important to realize that these tests are not designed to assess an overall level of ability. To do this, a different kind of test (norm-referenced) must be used. This sort of test is usually only administered by a psychologist, as explained in the previous chapter. Norm-referenced tests are divided into a number of different sections, which can be looked at individually or combined to give a measure of the child's general ability.

ATTENDANCE AT A PRE-SCHOOL GROUP

Your intervention team or child development centre will usually provide information about different pre-school groups. Other parents are also useful sources of information. In some cases, your interventionist or child development centre may be able to arrange for your child to be accepted preferentially at a pre-school group because of his special needs. There are basically two kinds of pre-school groups: 'parent and child' groups and 'pre-schools'. The latter term covers the various forms of day nurseries, crèches, nursery schools, and kindergartens for pre-school-aged children.

Parent and child groups

These are groups that parents attend together with their infant or toddler. The aim is for parents to have a chance to meet one another and share experiences. The children have an opportunity to mix with one another and play with different toys.

You may have a choice of going to an ordinary group or to a special group run for children with special needs. The decision concerning which to attend is a personal one. Some parents prefer to be in an environment where the children are not disabled, while others find that they receive more appropriate advice and encouragement at a special group. Some parents attend both.

Pre-school centres

Unlike the parent and child group described above, at a pre-school centre parents do not usually remain with their child.

Fig. 19. Johnny, aged 5 years, at pre-school.

Whether your child attends a pre-school centre should be a personal decision. Many parents are able to give their young child with Down syndrome a perfectly adequate learning environment at home. Nevertheless, many feel that involvement in a regular routine, with other children to observe and imitate, assists their child's development. Some pre-school-aged children with Down syndrome crave the company of other children, and may appear bored with the home routine. While many children with the syndrome quickly adjust to school without having gone to a pre-school centre first, others seem to benefit from this preparation for school.

Most children with Down syndrome cope well in an ordinary pre-school setting (Fig. 19). Often it is best to have the assistance of an interventionist who helps integrate the child into ordinary pre-school activities. He or she will advise the pre-school teacher on how to ensure that the child is included in activities.

Early school enrolment

There are a small number of children with Down syndrome who, because of a more significant intellectual disability or immaturity in behaviour, do not cope well at an ordinary pre-school centre. These children may benefit from enrolment at a special pre-school centre, if this is possible in their area.

Many special schools have classes for children of pre-school age. These classes often provide the structured programme and contained environment that suit some young children with Down syndrome. Schools, both ordinary and special, are discussed in the next chapter.

12. Which school?

All children with Down syndrome benefit from appropriate schooling. In addition to gaining new skills at school, children with Down syndrome usually enjoy the company of other children, the familiarity of the routine, and the rewards of learning.

Much of the knowledge that normal children acquire simply by watching and taking part in the world, children with Down syndrome need to be taught in a systematic way. Making purchases, travelling, cooking, interacting appropriately with others, and caring for oneself, are skills which normal children pick up as they go along. Children with Down syndrome often have to be taught these vitally important skills in order to gain the greatest degree of independence later on.

In order for your child to derive the maximum benefit from her education, the school you choose must meet her individual educational and social needs. In this chapter, I shall guide you through the different educational options available to children with Down syndrome.

A WIDENING WORLD

Sending a child off to school usually gives rise to mixed feelings in parents. On the one hand, there is the excitement of entering a new phase in the child's life, with the promise of new achievements. On the other, parents may feel resentful that the control of much of their child's learning and behaviour must be handed over to others. You will need to guard against allowing this natural response to get in the way of an appropriate education for your child. It is best to regard yourself, the teachers, and the other professionals involved in your child's education, as a team. Each member of the team plays a part in providing the best education for your child. It is essential that you and other members of the team should communicate regularly. It is a good idea to have a 'communication book', which your child takes with her to school each day. In it, you and the teachers

Fig. 20. David, aged 7 years, in a language class.

can exchange information on a daily basis. You should not
hesitate to request a meeting with your child's teacher if there
is something that is causing you concern. Do this as early as
possible.

CHOOSING AN EDUCATIONAL PLACEMENT

It is important to realize that every child with Down syndrome
has different educational needs, and that these needs change
with time. A placement that is right for one child will not
necessarily suit another. Any placement should be regarded as
temporary, and kept under review. Ignore well-meaning advice
from people who do not know your child's individual needs.
Statements such as 'Put him into the local ordinary school like I
did with my child', or 'Special schools are best', should be
treated with caution.

When a school has been recommended by the assessment
team, arrange a visit to see it for yourself. It is a good idea, if
possible, to have a professional accompany you on a visit to a
school. A social worker or intervention teacher may be willing.
Such a person may be helpful, as parents often forget to ask

important questions during a school visit. You can also discuss your impressions with this person after the visit, to help you make up your mind about the suitability of the school for your child.

When evaluating an educational placement, try to put yourself in your child's position. Where would she be happiest? Where would she learn the most useful skills? On your visit, make sure you see the class your child will be entering. Will she get on with the children? Will she enjoy and benefit from the work? Look at the layout of the school. Will she manage the stairs? Will she be safe in the playground?

Whatever placement you eventually decide upon, it is unlikely to be perfect. Schools rarely are. What you need to find is the best alternative for your child at that stage. Always keep in mind that no placement needs to be permanent. Regular reviews should be undertaken, and your child can move to a more appropriate class or school if her needs are found to have changed.

EDUCATIONAL OPTIONS

There are eight possible settings in which a child with Down syndrome can be educated. These are listed in Table 5. Not all these options are available in every area, and you will need to discuss which local placement options are available with the person who carries out the pre-school assessments.

These different settings are unfortunately sometimes referred to as a 'ladder' system of special education. This gives the impression of a hierarchy, with some options higher up on the ladder than others. This is not the case. Each setting provides its own unique advantages (and disadvantages). The best option for any child is the one which provides that particular child with the greatest advantage in the least restrictive environment. The existence of a number of options allows the child to move to another setting, should her needs change. The options are as follows:

1. Ordinary class

This is only appropriate for a small number of children with Down syndrome. It should be remembered that teachers in an

Table 5. Educational options

---
1. Ordinary class
2. Ordinary class with consultant
3. Ordinary class with itinerant special teacher
4. Ordinary class with withdrawal to a resource room
5. Special class plus part-time ordinary class
6. Full-time special class in ordinary school
7. Full-time special day school
8. Residential special school

---

ordinary class generally do not have special-education training, and usually have little time to help a child with special needs. Unless the class is unusually small (approximately ten children), a child with Down syndrome would only benefit from an ordinary class if she were able to learn at an average pace. The child should also fit in socially with the normal children, to obtain the greatest benefit from this placement. Such a class may be suitable for the first year or two of schooling, after which, if the child's special needs can no longer be met, another option should be considered.

It is great pity to see a child with Down syndrome in an ordinary class which is not catering to her needs, and where integration, in fact, merely becomes window-dressing. Such a child is wasting her school years. While the rest of the class cruises ahead, she falls behind, and her self-esteem plummets.

2. Ordinary class with a consultant

In this situation, the classroom teacher is able to consult a special educator about the best ways to help the child with Down syndrome in his or her class. The classroom teacher does not generally have special-education training, but by meeting with a consultant on a regular basis, he or she can receive advice about helping the child with Down syndrome.

This option is generally preferable to that mentioned above, but still requires an educationally and socially competent child, able to function very close to the average level. This is especially so if the class has more than about twenty pupils, as is the case in most schools.

3. Ordinary class with the help of an itinerant special teacher

An itinerant teacher visits a school at certain times during the week. Unlike the consultant mentioned above, who merely advises the class teacher, an itinerant teacher will actually teach the child on a one-to-one basis. If there is more than one child with special needs, these children may be taught in a small group, either in the classroom or in a separate room.

The itinerant teacher tends to reinforce those things that the ordinary classroom teacher is teaching. He or she may also extend the curriculum to include self-help and social skills, important to the child with Down syndrome.

This system can be a difficult one to arrange. Itinerant teachers are usually in short supply, and are often not able to spend sufficient time with children with special needs. As the child will still be spending most of her time in the ordinary classroom, she will need to fit into that environment educationally and socially.

If you are interested in an itinerant teacher for your child, find out from the principal whether you or the school can apply for funding for such a teacher.

4. Ordinary class with withdrawal to a resource room

This option describes the situation where the child regularly spends part of every day in a resource room with a specially trained teacher, and the rest of the day in an ordinary classroom. This is a very successful way of integrating a child into an ordinary class, while still providing special help, and suits some children with Down syndrome who have a borderline or mild degree of intellectual disability.

It is usually only possible to set up a resource room if there are a number of children with special needs in one class. The person who does the pre-school assessment will be able to direct you to such a class, if it is suitable for your child.

5. Special class plus part-time ordinary class

In this situation, most of the school day is spent in a special classroom within an ordinary school. The children in the special class do most of their academic work in that environment, and join an ordinary class for physical education, singing, domestic science, and other less academically demanding activities.

Children who are not usually good at mixing with normal children may be able to do this better when part of a special-class group, than on their own. In the small special class, the children get a great deal of individual attention, and the benefit of an appropriate curriculum.

Many parents feel that this arrangement provides their child with the best of both worlds, and gives less capable children an opportunity to come into contact with normal children.

There are an increasing number of special classes, catering for children with a wide range of abilities and some specific learning difficulties. If you are interested in a special class, make certain that you visit one that is appropriate for your child.

6. Full-time special class in an ordinary school

This option is sometimes available for children with more severe degrees of disability. The child spends her time in a special classroom in an ordinary school, coming into contact with the normal children during playtime and before and after school. In contrast with the previous option, joint classes with the normal children are not part of the programme.

7. Full-time special day school

Some children do not manage the hurly-burly of the ordinary school. They may be disruptive, or need a very structured and contained environment in order to feel secure. Special schools may provide the best environment for such children. These children often benefit from the fact that they fit in to their own class and the school as a whole.

Such schools can often provide support, in the way of therapy, parent groups, and outings, which is often difficult to arrange for children in an ordinary school. There is more opportunity for the child's self-esteem to be enhanced, as she is one among equals in this school environment, rather than being one of the less capable students in an ordinary school.

The special school curriculum emphasizes practical matters,

such as using public transport, cooking, and personal hygiene. Even though the child with Down syndrome may have difficulty in reading sentences, she may be taught to read 'survival' words, so that she can manage to travel on public transport and follow directions. There will usually be many opportunities for going on outings, and for practising shopping transactions and possibly more complicated procedures, such as filling in bank forms. Children who have difficulty with arithmetical functions may be taught to use a calculator. During their senior years at a special school, pupils are usually given vocational guidance. Most special schools also have a work-experience programme for pupils in their last few years at school.

If a child with Down syndrome is having difficulties which need the help of a physiotherapist, speech therapist, or occupational therapist, this is generally available in a special-school setting.

The environment in a special school is more secure for a child with a poor sense of danger. Close supervision, particularly in the playground, helps to prevent a child becoming lost or hurt. Sporting activities during school hours will be appropriate, given the physical limitations of children with intellectual disability.

A special school also provides more back-up for teachers, so that they are less isolated in managing specific problems, particularly those related to children's behaviour. Such schools often provide appropriate sex education for children, with parental permission. Many parents find that a special school provides them with an opportunity to meet other parents who have similar problems.

One of the main concerns parents have about sending their child to a special school is that she will copy the abnormal mannerisms of other children at the school. It should be realized that, in most special schools, children are streamed into classes according to ability, and your child is likely to be with children of similar abilities. While it is true that some children do imitate unwanted mannerisms, with correct behaviour management techniques, such behaviours usually go away. Children pick up undesirable behaviours from other children even in ordinary schools.

Special schools may be government-run or privately run. Each one is different, and it is important for you to visit any special school which is recommended for your child, so that you can assess it yourself. Children are usually grouped according to ability, and there may be a lot of variation in ability between different classes. Make sure you see the actual class that your child will attend.

8. Residential special school

In the same way that some parents send their normal children to boarding school, there are residential special schools for children with intellectual disability. The children often spend the days and nights during the week at the school, and return home each weekend. Such schools may be of benefit to children who are having difficulty learning to be independent in the home environment, or whose behaviour is causing stress and disruption to the family.

PRIVATE (NON-GOVERNMENT) SCHOOLS

Ordinary private schools are often willing to take a child with an intellectual handicap, although, unfortunately, many do not cater for the special needs of such a child. If you want your child to go to an ordinary private school, you should visit and find out exactly what kind of education and what kind of environment your child will be in. How many children will there be in the class? What is the curriculum? Will there be any special help available for your child? You will also need to find out how your child's progress will be monitored. Some schools may provide a form of assessment; or you may need to continue with independent assessments from a child development centre.

There are also some privately run special schools. One of the reasons that parents are attracted to such schools is that many are part of a 'whole of life' programme for children. Children who attend the school are able, as adults, to be accommodated in residential services provided by the organization that runs the school. They may also be able to work in workshops and activity centres run by such an organization. This is something parents need to consider early, as children may not be accepted by such organizations after a certain age.

Before becoming involved with a private school or organization, always find out what voluntary work you will be expected to do. Some private schools expect a great deal of parental involvement and fund-raising.

REGULAR REVIEWS OF A CHILD'S PLACEMENT

Annual reviews of a child's educational placement are a legal requirement in some countries. If you can, always try to attend such reviews, and make certain that your own feelings are known. Do not be confused by jargon, and insist that any technical terms are explained. Approach the review in a spirit of goodwill, but do not be afraid of asserting yourself.

INDIVIDUAL EDUCATION PROGRAMMES (IEPs)

In the USA, IEPs are part of the legal requirement of PL94–142. In other countries, a similar educational plan is often drawn up for each child, though it may be referred to by a different name. Whatever it is called, an educational plan for your child should be developed in consultation with you, the parents. It should outline, in clear and simple language, what your child has already achieved, and what objectives she is expected to reach.

SCHOOL TRANSPORT

Transport from home to school and back again is often provided for both special classes and special schools. You should find out whether this is available to your child by contacting the Education Authority. This is specially important if your child is to attend a special school or class a long distance away from home. Once she is older, she may be taught to travel independently to and from school, provided that she is capable of this and the journey does not involve unacceptable risks. Travel training is described in the next chapter.

13. Adolescence

Adolescence is a difficult time for parents of normal children, and is equally so for parents of children with Down syndrome. In most adolescents with Down syndrome, the physical changes of puberty occur at the same age as they do in normal adolescents. But in Down syndrome the hormonal changes and associated physical and emotional effects occur in a child who is immature intellectually, and who does not experience the rapid development of abstract thought that characterizes normal adolescence.

THE CHANGES OF PUBERTY

It is sometimes stated that boys and girls with Down syndrome reach puberty at an older age than other children. It is also stated that pubertal changes in individuals with Down syndrome are often incomplete. Such statements are based on surveys done in the past on individuals living in institutions. Recent surveys of adolescents with Down syndrome living at home have shown that the changes of puberty occur at almost the same average age as they do in individuals without the syndrome. Pubertal development also follows a normal pattern in these adolescents.

Early changes

Parents often do not realize that the hormonal changes of puberty start long before any of the physical changes are apparent in their child. Some two years before any outward indication, the small gland at the base of the brain, the pituitary, starts to produce substances which stimulate the ovaries in a girl, and the testes in a boy, to produce the appropriate sex hormones. For some time, no changes may be apparent in either growth or the development of the sex organs; but changes in the child's mood, and a tendency to restlessness or fatigue, may puzzle parents. This may happen as early as seven or eight years of age.

Physical development

Boys

The first visible change is the enlargement in the size of the testes. A short while later, the scrotum starts to become wrinkled. Pubic hair usually appears during the following year. The growth spurt begins at the time that the testes start to enlarge; but height does not increase markedly until later, when pubertal changes are more advanced.

During the next stage, the penis lengthens, and the small sacs where sperm is stored prior to ejaculation begin to enlarge and become filled with sperm. It is during this period that boys often have a night-time emission of sperm (wet dream), which is probably the body's way of coping with the sudden production of sperm.

Axillary (armpit) and facial hair develop late in puberty, and deepening of the voice is also a late event.

Many boys have some enlargement of breast tissue during puberty, sometimes on only one side. This may be associated with a tingling feeling or pain. It is a normal occurrence, and usually resolves spontaneously.

Girls

Girls develop on average two years in advance of boys. In a girl, the first visible changes are the appearance of breast buds and pubic hair. The growth spurt occurs at much the same time, but can precede these changes in some girls.

Sometimes, one breast enlarges more quickly than the other; but eventually both breasts reach roughly the same size.

The appearance of axillary hair occurs shortly after the appearance of pubic hair in most girls.

Menstruation is a relatively late event in pubertal development. It occurs, on average, eight months after the breast buds first appear. For most girls this would be at about twelve or thirteen. But there is much variation among different girls, and it is quite normal for the first period to start at any age between nine and seventeen. These first periods are often infrequent, and not associated with menstrual cramps. It takes, on average, fourteen months before a regular pattern is established. Menstrual cramps, if they are to occur, often do not start for a further two years.

Mood changes

The increased hormone levels in the blood that accompany puberty cause changes in behaviour. This may make the adolescent with Down syndrome more prone to fatigue. He may also be more irritable, and even show occasional outbursts of temper or defiance not seen previously. It often seems to parents that, regardless of what they do or say, they cannot win with their teenager. If you try to be patient and set consistent limits, you will be able to weather this stormy period until your child's behaviour settles down.

Clumsiness

With the rapid increase in growth that occurs during puberty, some parts of the body grow faster than others. There is a tendency for the adolescent to be out of proportion for a period of time. This results in some increased clumsiness, which eventually improves towards the end of this growth period. It is best to make some allowances for this clumsiness by altering your expectations, praising reasonable efforts, and giving sympathy for failures.

Increased appetite

With the rapid rate of growth that occurs during puberty, your child may start eating more. This is a normal part of puberty. You must make certain that your child's height and weight are regularly monitored during this time, as puberty is often associated with the onset of obesity in children with Down syndrome.

If it is clear that your child is becoming overweight, he should be checked by a doctor to exclude a hormonal cause. Thyroid gland deficiency, particularly, needs to be excluded in overweight children with Down syndrome. In the majority, however, the cause of obesity will be a combination of eating too much high-calorie food and inadequate exercise.

A reduction in the number of calories eaten is the basis of any attempt to control weight. In children who are growing rapidly, it is not always necessary to restrict calories to the point where weight is actually lost, unless the child is extremely overweight. It is usually sufficient simply to keep weight static, while allowing the child to grow taller, and thus become slimmer. Any weight-loss programme should be monitored by accurate measurements of the child's height and weight, which must then be plotted on a growth chart to observe trends, and compare these to average values. Merely looking at the weight is insufficient and misleading in a growing child.

There has been a change in attitude to diet over the past few years. Starches (complex carbohydrates), which were formerly thought to be fattening, are now the major component of a modern weight-loss diet. High-fibre intake is also beneficial, because the fibre takes a while to chew and gives a feeling of fullness. Fibre should be increased by eating foods which are naturally high in fibre, such as wholemeal cereals, fruit, and vegetables, and not by adding extracted fibre (for example unprocessed bran) to a diet in large amounts. Fat needs to be avoided; and this means being aware of hidden fat in some processed foods. Vegetable fats are no less fattening than animal fats. Sugars also need to be limited, and, once more, these are often hidden in processed foods. The best way to modify a diet is for all family members to make some changes to what they buy and eat. This does not have to be radical, and everyone can enjoy the low-calorie foods if they are gradually introduced.

It is often advisable to seek the advice of a qualified dietitian. Dietitians are based at most hospitals, and will see clients referred by a doctor. The dietitian can carefully go through a dietary history with the parents, and suggest modifications to the diet based on family preferences and routines. This is better than trying to adapt yourself to a particular diet which does not suit your family.

For older overweight children with Down syndrome, organizations such as 'Weight-Watchers' can provide an atmosphere of mutual support and encouragement, as well as a social outlet.

Exercise is also an important part of any weight-loss and weight-maintenance programme. Exercise should be enjoyable, and you should look for things that the child already enjoys doing and try to increase these activities. Swimming is often a good exercise for children with Down syndrome, and so is moving to music (aerobics). Weight-lifting, push-ups, and somersaults are not advisable for people with the syndrome.

Body odour

With the hormonal changes of puberty, cleanliness becomes an important issue for the adolescent. You will notice that the changes in the sweat glands mean that perspiration now has a stronger odour. Adolescents with Down syndrome need to be taught how to wash carefully, particularly under the arms, and to use a deodorant. Although many children with Down syndrome do not use soap during their pre-pubertal years, because of their dry skin, soap becomes necessary during puberty. A moisturizing cream such as Sorbolene with 10 per cent Glycerine can be used after bathing to prevent dryness.

Boys who are uncircumcised should be taught to follow a routine of cleaning under the foreskin to prevent odour and infection.

Girls should have their attention drawn to the problem of odour during periods, and be encouraged to bathe or shower more frequently at this time.

A TIME TO LEARN

Achieving maximal independence is one of the main goals of growing up for all children. Normal children learn many skills without needing to be taught. They watch and learn from what they see. As they reach adolescence, they start demanding more independence, and few parents are able to or want to deny them this.

The child with Down syndrome, on the other hand, needs to be taught many everyday skills, and given ample opportunity to practise them. Children with the syndrome often do not make the same demands for independence, and many parents, aware of their child's vulnerability, do not give him the opportunity to develop skills that are important for his independence. It is understandable to feel protective towards a child with an intellectual disability. Often, parents convince themselves that when the child is older, they will allow him more independence. But the process of achieving independence for a child with Down syndrome is a slow series of steps, which he must take over a period of time, starting from early childhood. It is wrong to think that a child who has been protected from having to do things for himself will be able to manage on his own as an adult.

As your child develops, you will not be able to protect him from all risks. Try to minimize these, but do not do this to the point where you restrict your child's ability to live as independent a life as possible.

Adolescence is a time when you can increase your child's range of experience, and teach him many new things about himself and those around him. Here are some of the things he should learn and some advice on how you can help him.

Teaching your child about sexuality

Many parents put off teaching about sexuality, in the belief that their child is 'not yet ready'. Teaching about sex does not require sitting your child down and having a formal talk with him. Parents teach by their attitude to their own bodies and sexual matters. Sexual education should be seen as part of a child's overall education. As he enters puberty, and has more independence in his social life, he needs to be taught more about sexual matters. Teaching has to be simple and repetitive, with the use of pictures. Dolls and videos are also useful teaching aids. Aim to teach a little at a time.

Schools often run courses in sex education, or you may contact the Family Planning Association (Planned Parenthood Federation in America and Canada), who supply literature and run courses. If your child attends such a course, you should try to be present, so that you can discuss with him what he has learnt.

When talking about sexual matters to your child with Down syndrome, always speak simply and give practical information. You do not need to give reasons or detailed explanations. Use the simple anatomical terms for parts of the body, such as 'penis' and 'vagina'. Avoid using words that are difficult to pronounce ('periods' is much easier than 'menstruation'). Try to make your child aware of the meaning of alternative terms that he may come across, even if you do not use them yourself.

Managing menstruation

Most adolescent girls with Down syndrome manage their menstruation very well. Any girl who is able to go to the toilet independently should be able to learn to change her own sanitary pad, and mothers should encourage their daughters to become independent in this regard. Your daughter will find this easier if she is prepared for menstruation early, by about the age of nine.

Detailed information is unnecessary. Rather, give her practical advice about what signs to look for, and reassure her that her mother will be around to help. She should be told to inform someone she knows, either you or her teacher, when she first sees blood on her panties. She will have to be shown how to use a sanitary pad, and this should be demonstrated a number of times. She will also need to understand that this is something that is done in private, and that she should not remove her pad and show it to anyone. Make certain she knows how to dispose of a soiled pad.

It is important that you speak in a positive way about menstruation, avoiding words such as 'the curse' or 'being unwell'. When she has her first period, tell her that you are delighted that she has taken this first step towards womanhood, and mark the event by giving her an appropriate gift.

Masturbation

Masturbation is a normal way of releasing sexual tension for both boys and girls. Initially, the young adolescent with Down syndrome may not understand that this is something that should be done in private. He may be so unaware of appropriate social constraints that he may wish to draw attention to his erect penis.

Parents are often dismayed, believing that this behaviour represents some sort of sexual deviancy. It is simply a matter of lack of awareness, due to the fact that the child is intellectually less mature than his body would suggest. Adolescent children with Down syndrome usually understand sexual matters as a five- or six-year-old would. They are often at a stage of intense curiosity, and have not yet developed the modesty that comes with slightly more advanced mental development. When your child behaves inappropriately, you may understand this behaviour better if you think of it in this way.

Explain that masturbation is something that should be done in private, and that one should not touch the breasts or genitals of others. Try not to react too strongly to inappropriate behaviour, as it will invariably subside after a period of time.

Over-reaction on the part of parents or siblings tends to set up a situation where the child continues to display the behaviour simply for the effect it creates.

Any child who is masturbating frequently should be examined by a doctor to exclude infection of the genitals, as this may cause the child to scratch or rub the genital area for relief.

Excessive masturbation is often associated with boredom. Try to find activities to occupy your adolescent if this seems to be a problem.

It should be noted that a particular medication, thioridazine (Melleril), used occasionally as a tranquillizer in people with Down syndrome, will stop males from ejaculating. This side-effect should be kept in mind if sexual frustration occurs in a male on this medication.

Your child's social development

Adolescence is a time for increasing your child's range of experience. It is often at this stage that he can start attending social clubs. Many adolescents enjoy the company of other similarly disabled people at a regular 'coffee club', 'disco', or excursion.

Adolescents need to socialize with other adolescents, and not exclusively with younger children or adults. It is important that they have a chance to mix with other adolescents of the opposite sex as well. Social clubs, respite-care cottages, sports activities, and holiday camps may all provide an appropriate opportunity (see Chapter 9). Discos and social clubs need supervision, and a young adult worker is usually the most acceptable supervisor for an adolescent group.

When your adolescent goes out, make sure he has some form of identification, such as his name and address written on a card, and some money to get home or make a telephone call.

Your child's clothes and general appearance should be fashionable and appropriate for his age. Keep an eye on what other adolescents are wearing so that you can advise him about suitable clothing and grooming.

Travel training

Adolescence is also the stage when children can learn more independence in travelling. In many cities, independent travel may be hazardous even for a competent adult. You will need to judge for yourself whether independent travel is appropriate. Members of the mental handicap team, or your child's teacher, may help with a travel-training programme. This usually means carefully deciding upon a particular route, for example, from home to school, planning how the child will get there, and then going over the trip with him. Initially, he should be accompanied. When it is clear that he understands what to do, he should be sent on his own, with someone following him without his knowledge. This will allow you to make certain that he is able to manage the trip. It is important to carefully rehearse what would happen in the case of an unexpected occurrence (such as a train not arriving on time). It is also helpful to try to 'stage-manage' such unexpected occurrences, while shadowing your child, so that you can observe his response.

You will always have to keep in mind that living means taking risks, and that you will need to take many calculated risks if your child with Down syndrome (or any child for that matter), is to achieve greater independence. It is much better to do this in a gradual way, so that the child is not suddenly put in the position of needing to take risks without having been prepared for them.

Preventing sexual abuse

Individuals with intellectual disability are, unfortunately, often vulnerable to sexual abuse. As a parent, ensure that your child understands that there are acceptable and unacceptable ways of being touched. Teach him to say 'no' to unacceptable touching, and to move away. Tell him about sexual abuse in a straight-forward manner, so that he will recognize it if it occurs, and hopefully tell you about it. Make certain he knows not to go off with strangers.

If you notice a sudden change in your child, such as a reluctance to be with a certain person, withdrawn behaviour, a reappearance of bedwetting, or physical signs such as irritation about the genitals or anus, you should suspect sexual abuse. Discuss this with your doctor, or contact your local child protection agency or the child-abuse unit at your nearest hospital.

Teaching children with intellectual disability to protect themselves against sexual harassment can be difficult. Two techniques which you may find useful are the ' "What if. . . ?" game' and the 'Circles of social distance'.

The 'What if. . . ?' game

This game is described by Michele Eliot in her book 'Preventing Sexual Assault' (Bedford Square Press). The parent asks the child a series of questions which start with the phrase 'What if. . . ?'. A good starting question would be 'What if you saw fire coming from the house next door?'. The questions can eventually become more difficult, such as 'What if a baby sitter wanted you to play secret games?' In each case, further questions are asked, until it is established that the child understands what constitutes an appropriate response. The child should understand that he has the right to say 'No!'.

Circles of social distance

This method of teaching appropriate social behaviour was developed by Marklyn P. Champagne and Leslie Walker-Hirsch. It is described here in a modified form:

The parent or teacher draws five concentric circles on a piece of paper. Each circle is shaded a different colour. The child is told that the centre is the 'self circle', the next circle is the 'family circle', the next the 'friend circle', the next the 'acquaintance circle', and the outermost circle, the 'stranger circle'. The circles can then be referred to by their individual colours to make it easier to remember. Each circle represents a different degree of social distance, and a different level of acceptable contact. The 'self circle' is the child himself: he can touch himself as he pleases. The 'family circle' represents close relatives, who can be hugged and kissed. The 'friend circle' represents good friends, who can be waved to and hugged. The 'acquaintance circle' refers to those people whom the child knows or is introduced to, but is not friendly with: acquaintances may be greeted with a handshake, but that is all. Lastly, there is the 'stranger circle': strangers should not touch or be touched in any way.

It is important that these degrees of social distance should be consistently adhered to, or the child will become confused. For example, it is inappropriate to ask your child to say 'goodbye' to a professional, such as a teacher or doctor, with a kiss, no matter how fond he may be of the person. He needs to learn that a handshake is appropriate for such an acquaintance.

Telling your child about his disability

Adolescence is often the time when children with Down syndrome first ask their parents why they are different from other children. As in the case of sex education, you should not wait for your child to ask questions before raising the subject.

Children start comparing themselves to their peers from an early age, long before they can ask questions or understand explanations about individual differences. From the time he is young, you can help your child by praising his efforts, giving him many opportunities to succeed, and comforting him when he has failed.

As your child with Down syndrome nears adolescence, you should discuss his condition with him. Do not wait for him to first hear that he has a handicap or Down syndrome from someone else. Unfortunately, children often learn this first from another child, when the terms are used in a derogatory manner. Let him first hear these words from you, in a positive way. Explain that different people are talented in different ways. Point out those things at which he is better, and the special qualities that he has. Then explain that some things are more difficult for him, even when he tries very hard. Acknowledge how frustrating this must be for him, but also point out the special ways in which some of his difficulties are being overcome. Use words such as 'handicap' and 'Down syndrome', so that he understands these terms. It is important to emphasize the wide variation among people with handicaps and with the syndrome, and to explain that he is an individual with his own unique attributes.

Adolescents and adults with Down syndrome occasionally form the mistaken impression that they are related to other people with the syndrome because of their physical resemblance. Help your child understand that he has a family of his own from whom he has inherited many of his characteristics, and that he is not related to other people with the syndrome.

Two books, 'I have Down's syndrome' by B. Pettenuzzo (Franklin Watts) and 'I have a mental handicap' by Althea (Dinosaur Books), are suitable for adolescents and adults with Down syndrome. The latter, although not dealing with the syndrome specifically, describes what it is like to have an intellectual disability in a sensitive and straightforward manner. It will help the older child and adult with Down syndrome gain a better concept of his disability and of his options for the future.

It is worth while bearing in mind that some children, once they know that they have a disability, use this as an excuse to avoid tasks that they dislike. You can quickly eradicate this form of manipulation if, from the outset, you draw a clear distinction between laziness and disability.

Helping your child cope with loss

No parents can protect their child from experiencing loss. Your child will inevitably experience loss, from something as minor as the loss of a favourite toy to the death of a loved one.

In the past, the need of people with intellectual disability to mourn was often ignored. Now, largely as a result of the pioneering work of Dr Sheila Hollins of St George's Hospital, London, there is a realization that children and adults with intellectual disability must be prepared for loss, and allowed to mourn a loss when it has occurred.

Adolescence is a good time to start talking to your child about growing old and dying. Most children with Down syndrome with a developmental age of about five to six years can grasp the concept of death. For most children with Down syndrome, this corresponds to a chronological age of about ten to twelve years. Later, at a developmental age of about nine or ten years, the universality of death, that is, the fact that it comes to everyone, can be grasped. Take the opportunity of the death of an animal, or someone the child knows, to talk about death to your child. 'The body book' by Claire Rayner (G. Whizzard/André Deutsch), has an excellent section on growing old and dying, which is easy to understand.

When a child or adult with Down syndrome loses a loved one, he should be given an opportunity to mourn. He needs to attend the funeral, to have ample opportunity to discuss his feelings, and to have something to remember the person by. With time, he will adjust to the loss, but will still need opportunities to speak about it and to make symbolic gestures, such as visits to the grave-side.

14. Adulthood

People with Down syndrome are living longer, healthier lives. Many people with the syndrome are now living into their fifties and sixties. The quality of their lives has also changed. Opportunities for adult education, leisure, employment, and accommodation have all increased. With many talented and energetic people working towards a fuller, more integrated life in the community for people with intellectual disability, there seems little doubt that the prospects for the future will be even brighter.

LOOKING AHEAD

Parents of infants and young children with Down syndrome invariably wonder what their child will be like when she reaches adulthood. It is only natural that you should be concerned about your child's future. But it is no easier to predict what a particular infant with Down syndrome will be like when she reaches adulthood than it is to make the same sort of prediction about a normal infant. There are so many factors which play a part: the child's temperament, upbringing, and intelligence, and the particular opportunities which are available to her when she reaches adulthood, all influence the sort of person she will be.

Adults with Down syndrome vary tremendously in temperament and ability. They always need more help to get by in the community than the average person. The amount of help may vary from needing someone to assist with financial matters and dealing with bureaucracy, to those individuals who need constant assistance. While it is impossible to predict what sort of adult a particular infant will eventually be, most adults with Down syndrome are able to take some responsibility for their daily needs, and require intermittent rather than constant supervision.

TREAT HER LIKE AN ADULT

A person with Down syndrome has two 'ages': her actual (chronological) age and her mental age. The latter refers to her level of mental functioning. Mental age is only a very rough concept. While it is true that an individual's understanding of the world and her social and self-help skills may be similar to those of a younger person, her responses will have been modified by her greater experience of life.

In the past, parents were often told to treat their adult son or daughter with Down syndrome according to his or her mental age. This meant that adults with the syndrome were often dressed, spoken to, and organized as if they were children. In the sixties, there was a reaction to this, and other aspects relating to the care of people with disabilities, in the form of a philosophy called 'normalization'. This was initially formulated by Bank-Mikkelsen in Scandinavia, and further developed by Wolfensberger in the USA. These workers reassessed the manner in which people with intellectual disability were treated, and advocated that this should be done in a way appropriate to their chronological age. The adult with Down syndrome should be dressed like anyone else of her age, with a modern hair style and fashionable clothes. She should be introduced to someone as 'Miss Mary Smith', rather than 'Mary'. Her recreational activities should be those that are 'normal' for someone of her age. In addition, she should, wherever possible, use ordinary services and facilities.

This normalization principle has resulted in many improvements in the quality of life for individuals with Down syndrome and other intellectual disabilities. There is now greater acceptance in the community of both children and adults with intellectual disability.

Some allowance should always be made for the disability of a person with Down syndrome, and adult behaviour should not be too stringently defined. It is worth remembering that normal adults indulge in certain childish pursuits. For example, before discouraging an adult with Down syndrome from collecting teddy bears, it should be remembered that many normal adults collect things that children also collect, such as stamps and coins. Adults with Down syndrome should be allowed to ex-

perience the adult freedom to enjoy harmless pursuits, even if
they are sometimes childish.

HOW MUCH LEGAL CONTROL DO
PARENTS HAVE?

Parents are often surprised to discover that after their child
with Down syndrome reaches the age of eighteen years, they
cease to be her legal guardians. After that age, parents no longer
have the power to make decisions for their child, or the legal
right to sign documents on her behalf. Parents can, of course,
continue to give guidance to their son or daughter after he or
she reaches adulthood, in the same way that they would for a
normal child. But the person with Down syndrome is entitled
to disregard parental advice.

When an adult with Down syndrome is able to make informed
decisions about her own affairs, parents can best help by
accepting her independence. When giving advice, make certain
you take into account the needs and preferences of your child.
If a dispute arises, you may enlist the help of a worker from the
community mental handicap team; but this can only be done if
your son or daughter is willing.

In the case of adults with Down syndrome who are unable to
understand their affairs, some form of protection is needed. In
many areas of life, such as education, training, employment,
accommodation, health care, marriage, and finances, such a
person is vulnerable to having her rights violated or ignored.
She may even be denied routine surgery on the grounds that
she is unable to understand the nature of the operation, and
hence to give informed consent.

It is clear that people unable to understand their affairs
should have someone to provide help. Most countries, including the USA, Canada, New Zealand, and certain states in
Australia, but with the notable exception of England and Wales,
have guardianship legislation to ensure that this is the case.
Guardianship legislation varies from country to country; but in
all, a group of experts is empowered to appoint a guardian, if
needed, for a person with intellectual disability. (In the USA
different levels of guardianship are recognized—guardians, con-
servators, and advisers).

The aim of guardianship is to provide positive support and

help to the person with intellectual disability in taking major decisions. The proceedings of the group of experts who appoint guardians are usually conducted with as little formality and legal technicality as possible, and take place in an informal meeting room. Any of the parties, including the person concerned, the applicant, and the proposed guardian, may appear in person or be represented by an agent. One of the important innovations of modern guardianship legislation has been to ensure that guardians are only appointed if necessary, and that guardianship can be limited to one issue, such as consent for surgery. Parents are often appointed as limited guardians; but anyone regarded as suitable by the guardianship tribunal can be appointed.

Unfortunately, England and Wales do not have this sort of legislation. A statutory provision for guardianship is only available to adults who qualify under the Mental Health Act of 1983. Most adults with Down syndrome do not qualify under the provisions of this act, which is essentially designed for people with mental illness. While the Court of Protection can deal with matters relating to the property of a person with intellectual disability, it has no jurisdiction over other affairs. In England there is thus a legal void concerning the civil rights of intellectually disabled adults who are unable to make informed decisions. The only legal forum for resolving any conflicts would be the formal and adversarial atmosphere of the courtroom. There seems little doubt that it is only a matter of time before legislation is passed to rectify this situation.

CITIZEN ADVOCACY AND SELF-ADVOCACY

A citizen advocate is someone who makes representations on behalf of an intellectually disabled person. An advocate should not be confused with a guardian. An advocate, unlike a guardian, cannot make decisions for a person with intellectual disability, neither can he or she sign a legal document on her behalf.

Parents are usually the advocates for their child with Down syndrome while she is young, but it is often worth while contacting a local citizen advocacy programme to obtain an advocate for your son or daughter once he or she becomes an adult. Someone from such a programme may have the energy and enthusiasm to take up issues on behalf of your son or daughter.

Citizen advocacy organizations are becoming increasingly common. In the UK, a number of organizations providing advocacy have banded together to form the Advocacy Alliance. You can usually find the name of the local office through your community mental handicap team.

There is now an awareness that some disabled people are able to speak for themselves with little help from a citizen advocate. This may be through creative projects such as drama or writing, or through committees and public meetings. A number of conferences have been organized in both the UK and the USA for people with intellectual disability, in which disabled people have spoken about topics they had chosen themselves. Disabled people now sit on some committees which deal with disability affairs, and there are newspapers produced by and for people with intellectual disability. Self-advocacy groups are increasing in number, and this field is continuing to expand.

INDIVIDUAL PROGRAMME PLANNING (IPP)

The importance of regular assessments during childhood was emphasized in Chapter 10. When adulthood has been reached, a system is needed to ensure that the disabled person's special needs are evaluated, and that plans are made to provide for these. It is important that planning should be individualized, and that the disabled person should be as fully involved with the decision-making as possible.

The process whereby the needs of an intellectually disabled person are assessed and goals are set to meet these is usually referred to as individual programme planning (IPP) or individual service planning (ISP). In some American programmes for adults with intellectual disability, IPP is a prerequisite for government funding.

The first step in IPP is to gather together those people who know the disabled person best. The disabled person herself should be included, as well as her guardian, advocate, and parents, and others who have regular contact with her. It is best if no more than about eight people attend, or the group becomes too large. Others can always be co-opted later if necessary. At the IPP meeting, one person takes the role of co-ordinator. The atmosphere should be relaxed, and all participants should be accorded equal status. Each person should be given a chance to report on their understanding of the special strengths and needs of the disabled person. The primary aim of all those concerned should be the best quality of life for the disabled person. All areas of the disabled person's activities should be reviewed. Her needs should be assessed according to priority, goals set, and responsibility delegated. The plan formulated should be written down, so that all those present receive a copy. One person should be chosen to co-ordinate the plan and ensure that it is implemented.

IPP meetings should occur regularly, usually every six to twelve months. You should always try to attend such meetings, as they provide an opportunity to meet people who come into regular contact with your son or daughter. They also allow you to share the responsibility of decision-making with others.

Recently there has been a move away from involving the disabled person directly in IPP meetings. Instead, the care co-ordinator or key worker attends the meeting, and acts as a 'broker', bargaining for resources on the person's behalf.

WHERE WILL SHE LIVE?

For many years, most adults with Down syndrome, (and many children too), lived in large institutions away from the rest of the community. This was done with the aim of protecting them from exploitation and neglect. For those parents who did not want their adult son or daughter to live in such an institution, the alternative was to keep him or her at home. This placed a great burden on parents, with the continual worry of what would happen to their child once they were no longer able to care for him or her.

Over the past few years, there has been a change in attitude to the needs of people with intellectual disability. It is now the policy in many countries to gradually close down large institutions, and provide cottages and sometimes hostels for small groups of people with intellectual disability. At the same time, it has been necessary to provide employment and recreational facilities for disabled people near to these homes, and to train and employ staff to provide supervision as needed. In some cases, 'half-way houses' have been established, where people with intellectual disability can receive training in skills such as cooking, laundering, and shopping, before moving into a group home.

It is understandable that many parents have mixed feelings about this move. While most would prefer a home in the community to a large institution, there are naturally fears about whether the intellectually disabled person's special needs for supervision and protection will be adequately met. Parents can be reassured that group homes can and do work, provided they are properly organized. There are many people with Down syndrome and other intellectual disabilities living in group homes in ordinary suburban and city houses all over the world, enjoying lives of dignity and freedom. This applies to people with a wide range of abilities.

In such houses, there are usually four or five intellectually disabled people. Each person has his or her own room, with his or her own possessions. During the week, he or she travels to work, either in open employment or in a sheltered workshop. Housework is shared. The person with Down syndrome is able to take part in any of the activities available to the rest of the community. She can visit the local park, the library, the cinema, the beach, the pub, or the church. She can visit friends, or attend a social club for disabled people. Support is provided in some form, which varies from someone who 'lives in' and does the cleaning and cooking, to someone who merely visits to supervise the successful running of the house. This is the person who would be called on if a problem arose.

Letting go

The time when an adult son or daughter leaves home to live in a group home or hostel is often an extremely difficult one for parent and child, and most parents will have many concerns about their child's future.

It is not the aim of parenthood to continue caring for your son or daughter throughout your life, but rather, to prepare him or her, during the childhood years, to live as independently as possible in adulthood. In the past, it was common for adults with Down syndrome to remain with their parents. Loving parents often looked after all the needs of their adult son or daughter. Eventually, when the parents became too ill or old to look after their child, he or she had received little or no preparation for living away from home. Many such people with Down syndrome were devastated to suddenly find themselves in a new environment, with no experience of coping without their parents.

It is far better if, during childhood, individuals with Down syndrome are prepared for eventual independence. They need to be taught to do as much as possible for themselves. Regular respite-care is an excellent preparation for eventual separation. Like anyone else, a person with Down syndrome should preferably leave home on reaching adulthood. She should move to a place of her own, such as a group home or hostel, if at all possible. The early days will be difficult for both the parent and child, but this type of planned change is much easier to adapt to than a sudden separation. The person with Down syndrome who has had a chance to adjust to separation gradually, will fare much better in the years ahead.

FURTHER EDUCATION

A great deal of emphasis is placed on early intervention in the education of children with Down syndrome. Attention has recently turned to development in the post-school period, and what may be called 'late intervention'. It is now being realized that learning is an activity which, for individuals with Down syndrome, should also continue beyond the school years. In addition to vocational training, people with Down syndrome need continued teaching in useful academic, self-help, and social skills.

More and more colleges of further education are realizing that people with intellectual disability need training after school. Courses cover such subjects as reading, writing, numeracy, self-advocacy, work skills, budgeting, leisure skills, and personal development. An adult with Down syndrome who has left school can often enrol in a course run by such a college, and consolidate and expand those things she learned during the school years. With the increased maturity of adulthood, it is often easier for her to gain some of the skills she did not have when she left school.

There are some special centres, such as Development Achievement Centres and Community Living Centres, which offer training specifically for intellectually disabled people.

Living-skills training courses sometimes start with a functional assessment of the person's abilities, and assistance is provided to teach everyday skills in the individual's normal environment. Some centres have equipment, so that cooking, laundering, etc., can be taught. There will also be follow-through to the home environment, so that the individual is able to make use of these skills in her normal surroundings. It is no use learning to load a front-loading washing machine if there is only a top-loader at home or at work.

The realization that adults with intellectual disability need to keep up and extend their learning after they leave school is relatively recent. It is hoped that, in the future, adult education for the intellectually disabled will be provided by all tertiary education centres, where adults with intellectual disability can learn in an environment conducive to adult education.

EMPLOYMENT

Every adult with Down syndrome should have the satisfaction of work, regardless of his or her capability. During the last years of school, the advice of someone experienced in vocational counselling should be sought. This may be someone situated in the child's school, a member of the community mental handicap team, or someone from a private or government vocational guidance agency. In making a decision about an appropriate vocation, the person's intellectual capability, as well as her temperament, ability to travel independently, and interests, and also the local opportunities should be taken into account.

Towards the end of high school, children with Down syndrome are often given the chance to have work experience, in order to learn how a particular job is done, and more importantly, about work itself: the travelling, the organizational structure, the daily routine, and how to interact with other workers.

There are three employment options available to people with intellectual disability: open employment, where the individual is employed in an ordinary job; sheltered employment, in a workplace specially organized for people with intellectual disability; and thirdly, for those adults without the skills needed for either of the above, the activity-therapy centre.

1. Open employment

Successful placement in open employment requires careful job selection, work-preparation, and support. Work experience should start during the last years of school. Many people with intellectual disability need time in a work-preparation centre before starting work. There are now an increasing number of schemes for helping intellectually disabled people succeed in open employment.

In the United Kingdom, the results of the Pathway Scheme sponsored by MENCAP (see Appendix) have been very encouraging. A 'pathway officer' seeks out a potential employer, and then identifies someone who will act as a support for the intellectually disabled person. Wages are paid at the usual rate, with MENCAP contributing half the amount. The support worker is also paid a bonus by MENCAP. Another United Kingdom option is the Manpower Services Commission (MSC), which will fund employment schemes that do not exclude people with intellectual disability. You can get more information from your local job centre or disablement resettlement officer.

In the USA, there are government-funded programmes providing help with job selection, training, and support. For information about such programmes, contact your local state Vocational Rehabilitation Agency. The address of your local agency can be obtained from your regional office of the US Department of Education (ask for Rehabilitation Services).

In Australia, the Department of Industrial Relations has Vocational Services branches, and the Commonwealth Employment Service (CES) provides advice and special assistance to people with disabilities.

2. Sheltered employment

Open employment is not always available for people with intellectual disability, particularly in these times of rising unemployment. Even when open employment is available, it may not provide the best environment for every adult with intellectual disability. In open employment, a disabled individual may be under great stress, socially isolated, open to exploitation, or in danger of losing her job when times become difficult. In many cases, sheltered employment is preferable.

Fig. 21. Ms Liz Palmer at work as a pre-school assistant.

There has been a gradual increase in the number of sheltered workplaces in most developed countries, together with an improvement in working conditions. As in all workplaces, there is a need for a compromise between the most ideal working conditions and productivity. A good sheltered workplace should be light, airy, spacious, and provide training and support for employees. There should be variety in the work performed by each individual, proper staff supervision, and opportunities and facilities for some socialization and recreation during breaks from work. Requirements for work should be fair and businesslike.

People with Down syndrome usually enjoy taking part in the productive activity of a workshop, and enjoy the social interactions with their fellow employees. Their status and self-image are enhanced tremendously by receiving their own pay cheque on a regular basis. You can help your son or daughter by fostering pride in his or her work and workplace.

3. Activity-therapy centres

The small number of individuals with Down syndrome who find work at a sheltered workplace too difficult, still benefit from a regular away-from-home experience. There is no reason why any person with Down syndrome should spend weekdays at home. Activity-therapy centres, or activity centres as they are sometimes called, provide less capable disabled people with a structure in which they keep busy and enjoy themselves, without needing to produce goods or provide services. People at an activity-therapy centre are occupied by tasks that are within their capabilities. These may involve moving or dancing to music, playing games, and co-operating in art and craft activities.

These centres are slowly undergoing a change, with more emphasis on training and less on simply keeping people occupied. In the United Kingdom, they are now often referred to as 'social education centres', an indication of the new emphasis on training and education. Some people who attend these centres may later graduate to a sheltered workshop.

LEISURE

Leisure means different things to different people. For some it is an opportunity to relax and do very little, for others it is a time for intense activity. Each individual needs to make her own decision about how she wants to spend her leisure time. There are now many recreational activities for people with intellectual disability, and some areas have recreation officers who can suggest appropriate activities. Some occupational therapists have an interest in leisure pursuits, and can provide useful information. You may also be able to obtain a newsletter which tells you about recreational activities in your area.

Some adults will continue to take part in recreational pursuits which they started as children. This is one of the reasons why teaching your child to occupy and enjoy herself on her own and with others should start in the early school years. (Some aspects of recreation in childhood are discussed in Chapter 9.)

The adult with Down syndrome will have an opportunity to make friends at work, and with the people she lives with in a group home. In addition, there are now a number of social clubs which run on a regular basis, and allow adults with a disability to meet. These are sometimes run by community mental handicap teams or religious and other community organizations.

The 'leisure buddy scheme' described in Chapter 9 is a way

in which adults with Down syndrome can be accompanied when taking part in recreational activities.

In the United Kingdom, MENCAP runs a network of social clubs (Gateway Clubs), as well as holiday services for adults with intellectual disability.

Adults with intellectual disability can take part in special activities for disabled people or may be able to participate in ordinary activities. Horse-riding, ten-pin bowling, and swimming are particularly popular. These activities have the advantage of being enjoyable without necessarily being competitive. Many adults with Down syndrome also enjoy activities such as movement to music and Yoga. Yoga is particularly helpful for anxious individuals. For those who are more energetic, dancing and aerobics can be a good way of burning off energy. For those with athletic skills, the Special Olympics offers a goal to work towards.

Hobbies provide the opportunity for self-reliance, and for meeting other people with similar interests. Adults with Down syndrome often enjoy collecting things such as stamps or coins. A collection of different kinds of pressed leaves or flowers is an example of an inexpensive collection, where obtaining the specimens can be very enjoyable. Gardening is a popular pursuit, and can be adapted for people with a disability.

SEXUALITY

In the past, the sexual needs of people with Down syndrome were often not considered. We now realize that adults with the syndrome have the same sexual needs as other members of the community. Like everyone else, their sexual desires vary in intensity, and individuals with Down syndrome may have a low sex-drive or a high sex-drive. Certainly there is nothing abnormal about their sexuality. It is sometimes stated that people with Down syndrome have a low sex-drive. This, however, is not based on any reliable research, and is not true of many people with the syndrome. The idea that people with Down syndrome are 'sexually over-active' or liable to harm anyone because of their sex-drive is also untrue. Such notions may have arisen because of the tendency in the past to deny that individuals with the syndrome had any sex-drive at all, so that any normal demonstration of interest in things sexual was regarded as deviant. Adults with Down syndrome were seldom

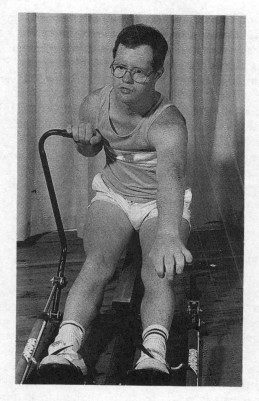

Fig. 22. Mr Bradley Thurgar, aged 21, exercises on his rower.

given an outlet for their sexual feelings, or the opportunity to learn what was appropriate sexual behaviour.

Individuals with the syndrome may at times appear to be engaging in abnormal sexual behaviour (such as touching strangers of the opposite sex in a suggestive way), because they have not been taught that this is unacceptable. When speaking to adults with intellectual disability, it is surprising to discover how little they have been told about sexual matters.

MARRIAGE

With the increasing tendency for adults with Down syndrome to live in group homes and hostels in the community, the likelihood of a person with Down syndrome marrying is increasing, and such marriages have happened in a few cases. Marriage as a stable, caring relationship between two individuals is clearly beneficial to disabled adults. As with any marriage, mistakes can be made and parental advice may be ignored.

In most cases, such marriages have taken place between a person with Down syndrome and another intellectually disabled person. Such partners often share a similar outlook on life. Marriages between individuals with Down syndrome and normal people have also occurred. Provided that this is a loving relationship and not based on pity or exploitation, there is a good chance that it will be successful.

HAVING CHILDREN

While marriage is certainly a way in which an adult with Down syndrome may reach fulfilment, having children is a more problematical issue. There are three aspects to consider: Firstly, are women and men with the syndrome fertile? Secondly, will the children be intellectually disabled? Thirdly, are people with the syndrome able to cope with the responsibilities of parenthood?

We know that women with Down syndrome can have children, although there is some evidence that their fertility is slightly less than normal. In such partnerships, if the male is normal, the theoretical chance of the child having Down syndrome is approximately ten per cent*. Yet in the 21 cases reported in medical journals of a mother with Down syndrome giving birth, ten (48 per cent) of the babies had the syndrome. This may reflect a greater tendency for doctors to report cases where the baby had the syndrome. If the male partner also has an intellectual disability, the chance of the child having a disability may be higher, depending on the cause of the father's disability.

In the case of men with Down syndrome, we know far less. This is because of the lack of opportunity, in the past, for males

---

* Half the women's eggs would have an extra chromosome, but approximately 80 per cent of pregnancies where the fetus has Down syndrome would be expected to end in spontaneous miscarriage.

with the syndrome to have children. It may also be related to the difficulty of proving paternity. There is only one report of a man with Down syndrome fathering a child; but there too the evidence of paternity is open to dispute. There is some research evidence to show that men with the syndrome have low sperm counts. This implies reduced fertility, rather than infertility. The fact that there are no irrefutable reports of a man with Down syndrome fathering a child does not mean that this could not happen. On theoretical grounds it would be expected that, if the female partner were normal, less than ten per cent of their children would have the syndrome.

Most surveys of families where one or both of the parents had an intellectual disability have found that these families experienced great difficulties. The children usually suffered from inadequate care, and the parents suffered from their inability to cope with the pressures of parenthood. This was so whether the children themselves were intellectually disabled or not.

It is important, therefore, to try to teach your child with Down syndrome that people can live together happily without having children. You should avoid making too much fuss of friends who are pregnant and of babies. It is also worth while trying to give your son or daughter some inkling of how difficult it is to look after a child. It is helpful if there is a younger brother, sister, cousin, or friend's child, to show that, in addition to being cute and cuddly, children can be difficult, demanding, and a lot of hard work.

For adults with Down syndrome who miss having a child, a substitute in the form of a pet or an opportunity to baby-sit for short periods may help to fill the void. Some adults with Down syndrome enjoy working as assistants in child-care centres, and satisfy an urge to nurture in this way.

Most importantly, you should ensure that your child is able to take effective contraceptive measures as an adult.

CONTRACEPTION

The adolescent with Down syndrome should be taught that sexual intercourse is an adult act. The idea of contraception should, therefore, be introduced to the young adolescent as a concept, with more detailed information given towards the end of the high-school years. Certainly, no young adult with Down syndrome should move into the work-force, whether that be in open or in sheltered employment, without having learnt the practicalities of contraception.

In the United Kingdom and Australia, the Family Planning Association gives excellent advice about contraception, and can recommend books, videos, and some of their own publications to aid in teaching about contraception. In the USA and Canada, a similar service is provided by the Planned Parenthood Federation.

Choosing a contraceptive

There is no 'best' method of contraception for people with Down syndrome. The choice of contraceptive method depends on the individual needs of the sexual partners. Advice should be sought from a family planning counsellor or the person's own doctor. The methods available are the condom, the 'pill', intra-uterine devices (IUDs), and hormone injections. Other methods of contraception, such as the diaphragm and spermicidal foam, have a high failure-rate in people with an intellectual disability, and therefore cannot be recommended.

If a condom is to be used, the man should be co-operative and disciplined, and will need to be taught how to obtain condoms and how to put one on. It is probably best to teach this using a model of a penis.

The contraceptive 'pill' should not be used in women with Down syndrome who have cyanotic (blue) heart disease.

If an intra-uterine contraceptive device is to be used, it is important that either the woman herself, or another person, checks that the strings of the device can be felt, by putting a finger into the vagina, after each period.

'Depo-provera' is the trade name of a hormonal contraceptive given by injection every three months. It has been the centre of controversy, with some authorities claiming that the possible side-effects, such as absent periods, uterine bleeding, and permanent infertility, make it unacceptable.

Sterilization

Sterilization is permanent contraception. It cannot be reversed. It can be performed on women (tubal ligation) or men (vasectomy). These operations should only be performed on an adult able to give his or her informed consent. In the case of an adult with Down syndrome who is unable to give informed consent, legal advice may be sought if it is thought that sterilization is the most appropriate form of contraception. In some countries, sterilization cannot be performed without informed consent.

Sterilization of young girls with Down syndrome used to be practised fairly commonly. Modern attitudes dictate that vulnerable girls should either not be put in a situation where they can be sexually taken advantage of, or another method of contraception should be used. When the girl is older, she can, if she is able, make her own decision about sterilization.

Hysterectomy

Hysterectomy (removal of the womb) was often used in the past as a form of sterilization and a means of stopping menstruation in women with Down syndrome. Hysterectomy is a major operation, and, with better methods of contraception available (including tubal ligation), it is no longer justified as a form of contraception. Women with Down syndrome can usually be taught to manage their own menstruation, and so hysterectomy to stop menstruation is rarely, if ever, necessary.

HEALTH IN ADULTHOOD

The health care of adults with Down syndrome deserves special mention. This is because a number of recent studies have shown that, while parents are very successful in ensuring good health-care for their young child with Down syndrome, adults with the syndrome often do not receive optimal care.

As discussed in Chapter 6, an adult with Down syndrome should have a number of regular health checks to detect specific problems that are more common in people with the syndrome. Vision and hearing should be tested every second year. Blood should be collected for thyroid testing every year, and people with Down syndrome should visit the dentist once a year.

Most adults with Down syndrome would not have had a neck X-ray during childhood to check for atlanto-axial instability. This is because of the fact that the association between these two conditions was not widely known before 1983. If an adult has not had an X-ray, this should be done before she takes part in any activity which puts her neck under strain (see Chapter 6).

In addition to these special checks, it should be borne in mind that adults with Down syndrome are susceptible to the same ageing diseases as other members of the community. Weight should be checked, and advice given concerning exercise and diet. Blood-pressure and blood cholesterol should be monitored regularly. Women with Down syndrome should have Pap smears on an annual basis, and should be taught how to examine their breasts, or have someone else examine their breasts for them.

Adults with Down syndrome are often disadvantaged in gaining access to a doctor, and may find it difficult to describe their symptoms when they are sick. For this reason, care must be taken in choosing a doctor. He or she must be prepared to give extra time to the person with Down syndrome, and make certain that she gets the best possible medical care. A community worker can play a useful role by helping a person with Down syndrome gain access to appropriate medical care, and by accompanying her on visits to the doctor.

GROWING OLD

You may be told or read that people with Down syndrome 'age prematurely'. This frequently quoted statement can be misleading. Ageing is a broad term, covering the many changes that occur in the body with time. There is no firm evidence that people with Down syndrome become more wrinkled, lose their hair, or develop any of the other outward changes of ageing, earlier than other people. With regard to changes such as atherosclerosis (hardening of the arteries) or osteoporosis (softening of the bones), there is also no evidence that these occur earlier in Down syndrome. While it is true that some studies of people with Down syndrome living in institutions have revealed changes related to advancing age (such as an increase in the amount of fat in the blood), it is likely that such changes reflect the life-style and diet associated with institutional life.

Ageing is a poorly understood process, which, while having a biological basis, is also influenced by environmental factors. Older people who have the opportunity to be physically active and intellectually stimulated, usually age more slowly. The effects of boredom and lowered self-esteem may mimic some of the changes associated with ageing. It is for this reason that studies of older people with Down syndrome who have led restricted lives in institutions should be treated with caution. Younger people with Down syndrome, now growing up with greater opportunities for a stimulating and rewarding life, may present a different picture when they reach old age.

There are three conditions which do, however, become more common as people with Down syndrome grow older. These conditions are Alzheimer disease, seizures, and changes in the immune system.

Alzheimer disease

Now that people with Down syndrome are living longer, it has become apparent that they are more likely than the general population to develop Alzheimer disease (named after Dr A. Alzheimer, a German physician, 1864–1915). This disorder, in addition to being more common in Down syndrome, may also occur at an earlier age.

Alzheimer disease is a condition which becomes more common as people grow older. It results in the forgetfulness, loss of skills, and confusion sometimes referred to as 'premature senility'. The onset is insidious, and often goes unnoticed. The first change is usually forgetfulness of recent events. In some people it may start with an apathy that leads to withdrawal from activities, and presents as depression. The progress of this disorder is often very gradual, and the person's condition may continue unchanged for some ten to fifteen years. In many cases it is mild, but severe forms, with significant deterioration in intellectual function and difficulties with physical activities such as walking and talking, may occur.

How common is Alzheimer disease in people with Down syndrome? To answer this question, a distinction must be drawn between changes brought about by Alzheimer disease in the brain that can only be seen under the microscope (pathological changes), and the intellectual and behavioural manifestations of the disease (clinical changes). Although studies have found the pathological changes of Alzheimer disease in the brains of all subjects with Down syndrome over the age of fifty years, *only one-third* of individuals with the syndrome over this age actually show evidence of intellectual or behavioural deterioration. The brains of people with Down syndrome are formed differently to those of other people, and the pathological changes of Alzheimer disease do not inevitably give rise to recognizable intellectual impairment in people with the syndrome.

Although the exact cause of Alzheimer disease is unknown, it has become clear that it is related to a combination of genetic predisposition and certain environmental factors. The exact nature of the environmental factors is unknown at present. Recent research indicates that there is a gene present on chromosome 21 which plays a part in the genetic predisposition to Alzheimer disease. In those people without Down syndrome who develop this disease, a duplication is sometimes found on one of their No. 21 chromosomes. People with Down syndrome are in a similar situation, because they have an extra dose of this gene as a result of its presence on their additional chromosome 21. This may explain why they are more liable to develop Alzheimer disease. A great deal of research is being undertaken in this area, and our understanding of Alzheimer disease, and its relationship to Down syndrome, should increase over the next decade.

In any person with Down syndrome who is suspected of having Alzheimer disease, treatable disorders which may cause the same manifestations should always be looked for. It is particularly important to exclude hypothyroidism (see Chapter 6), which is a treatable cause of confusion and behavioural disturbance. Psychomotor seizures (a form of seizure which may be confused with a behavioural disturbance) should also be excluded. It should also not be forgotten that people with Down syndrome, like the rest of the community, can develop psychiatric illness that may respond to psychotherapy and/or medication.

Seizures

A seizure (also known as a fit or a convulsion) occurs when the brain cells suddenly become overactive, and their normal working is interrupted. This may be regarded as a temporary 'short circuit' in the brain. If seizures become recurrent, the person is said to have 'epilepsy'.

Seizures are rare in children with Down syndrome; there is

some evidence that children with the syndrome are less prone to seizures than normal children. Once adulthood is reached, however, seizures become more common in people with the syndrome. At the age of fifty years, about one in ten people with Down syndrome will have had a seizure.

Seizures may take a number of forms. The most common is a *grand mal* seizure. During such a seizure, the person falls unconscious to the ground. Her body initially stiffens, and then the limbs jerk rhythmically for a period. Although this looks frightening to an observer, the person is in no pain. When the seizure stops, she may sleep for a period before recovering completely.

Once a person with Down syndrome has had a seizure, it usually indicates that she is prone to seizures, and needs to take medication for the rest of her life. In some cases, if the person has been seizure-free for a period of two-years, a slow withdrawal of the medication may be tried. This needs to be an individual decision. Anti-seizure medication should never be stopped suddenly.

A person who has had a seizure should wear a bracelet which states that she has seizures, and gives the name of someone who can be contacted in the event of a seizure. Most activities do not have to be curtailed in people who have seizures, but swimming should always be supervised.

Changes in the immune system

The immune system is that part of the body involved in fighting infection. Research has shown that, with increasing age, certain aspects of the immune system function less well in people with Down syndrome. This plays a part in making older people with the syndrome more susceptible to infection and malignancy. It also has the effect of encouraging antibodies to form against parts of the person's own body. As explained in Chapter 6, this is the mechanism for acquired hypothyroidism (Hashimoto thyroiditis). In addition, as people with Down syndrome grow older, diabetes and certain other hormonal deficiencies become more common, for the same reason. These problems should not be overemphasized. Although they are more common in people with Down syndrome than the general population, only a minority of people with the syndrome are affected.

15. Controversial treatments

The basis of modern management of Down syndrome consists of providing an appropriate education, a loving and caring family environment, and the measures to prevent and treat health problems outlined in Chapter 6. This approach has resulted in a considerable improvement in the abilities and health of children and adults with Down syndrome. Down syndrome, however, still cannot be cured.

BEFORE YOU BECOME INVOLVED

When there is no effective cure for a condition, numerous dubious 'cures' arise. The existence of a number of so-called 'cures' is usually a sign that no single one is effective. An effective treatment quickly displaces all others. Some parents of children with Down syndrome are understandably drawn towards those who claim they can cure the condition. It is often the most caring and loving parents who become involved. Unfortunately, some of these treatments may be harmful to the physical and psychological well-being of the child, and may be costly and time-consuming for the family as a whole.

It is important, therefore, that you carefully assess any treatment programme before becoming involved. Do not rely on stories of miraculous improvements and cures, but ask to see published evidence comparing children who have been treated with those who have not. Such experiments are called controlled trials, and should have been carried out 'blind', meaning that the person who assessed the children's performance did not know which had received the treatment and which had not, until after the assessments were completed. If the treatment consists of a medicine, the untreated group should have received a dummy medicine (placebo) to make the comparison valid. In addition, the person who carried out the trial should not have had a vested interest in the treatment.

An increasing number of independent trials of controversial treatments are now being reported in medical journals. In addition, government research bodies often make policy statements about certain treatments, based on reviews of scientific data. Your doctor will be able to obtain copies of these articles for you to study.

Discuss any proposed treatment with your doctor, and consider the reported advantages and disadvantages. Make certain that before starting any treatment, you decide upon what objective improvement you wish to see, and how long it should take before this occurs. If the objective is not achieved, treatment should cease. Do not allow yourself to accept some vague qualitative improvements decided upon at a later date. Be wary of ascribing every improvement to the treatment. Children with Down syndrome always develop new skills, and do so in sudden spurts followed by periods of consolidation. Their physical appearance also evolves over time, and their muscular tone gradually improves. Such changes are expected, and should not be ascribed to a particular treatment unless they are exceptional.

SOME CONTROVERSIAL TREATMENT PROGRAMMES

Cell therapy (Sicca cell therapy)

Cell therapy originated in Germany, and involves the injection of dried brain cells from lamb and calf fetuses into children with Down syndrome. The injections are usually given on a five- to six-monthly basis, although this varies from place to place. The children are also given a group of substances which includes vitamins, minerals, and thyroid gland extract.

The major proponent of this treatment is a German doctor, Franz Schmid of Heidelberg. The claims for this treatment are that it improves the child's general development, height, weight, head circumference, facial appearance, hair, and skin quality.

There is no sound theoretical reason why this treatment should work. The intellectual disability and physical appearance of children with Down syndrome are due to the way in which the brain and other parts of the body form in the womb, and there seems no reason why these should be changed by the injection of dead cells. A recent blind controlled trial carried out in Australia showed no significant differences in the developmental or physical characteristics of children with Down syndrome who were receiving cell therapy, compared with those who were not. Not only has the treatment no proven beneficial effect, but the injection of the foreign material on a regular basis may cause severe allergic reactions, which could result in death. In addition, there is concern that the animal cells could harbour viruses that may cause human disease.

The injection of dead cells in Down syndrome should not be confused with recent research suggesting an improvement in adults with Parkinson disease, following implantation of *live* brain tissue from human fetuses. Unlike Down syndrome, Parkinson disease is not due to abnormal formation of the brain prior to birth. It occurs when a certain substance required for normal brain function becomes deficient in parts of the brain during adulthood. In the treatment of Parkinson disease, the fetal brain tissue is alive, and continues to survive after implantation, producing the deficient substance. Such brain implants may be used in the future for conditions involving the brain, such as Alzheimer disease and Korsakoff psychosis, both of which start in adulthood.

Plastic surgery

Plastic surgery can be performed to change the appearance of children with Down syndrome. These operations have been carried out since the mid-1960s. Whether a changed appearance is advantageous is something that each child and his parents need to decide for themselves. Surgery causes pain and distress, and is not without risk.

Silicone implants can be inserted under the skin to build up the bridge of the nose, the cheeks, and the chin. These are usually relatively minor procedures, requiring a general anaesthetic and a couple of days in hospital. Parents have generally been pleased with the results. It is important to realize that the bridge of the nose, cheeks, and chin all grow with the child, and such operations should be deferred until after puberty, when the child will be better able to understand the implications of the operation.

Epicanthic folds usually get taken up as the nasal bridge grows or, in the case of the surgery described above, when a silicone implant is inserted. Epicanthic folds can be surgically removed if they persist after puberty. Protruding ears can also be operated on. This is a relatively common operation, which has a high success rate.

An operation to remove part of the tongue became popular in the early 1980s. As mentioned earlier, some children with Down syndrome have a habit of protruding their tongues. They can often be taught to keep their tongues in their mouths, using the method described in Chapter 8. There is a proportion of children, however, in whom the habit persists. If the large tongue is unsightly, a tongue-reduction operation may be considered. The operation is probably best left until it is clear that the tongue is a problem, which is usually after four years of age. Unlike the silicone implants and removal of epicanthic folds discussed above, this is a major surgical procedure. The tongue is a vascular, mobile organ, and complications, such as infection, wound-opening, and obstruction to breathing may occur during the first four to six weeks after the operation, when the tongue is very swollen. Some of the taste organs on the tongue are removed during the operation, and so a decrease in taste sensation occurs. As many as one-third of parents have reported reservations about the results of the operation. Improvement in speech clarity rarely occurs, and speech may be worse in as many as one in ten children after the operation. This means that, if the operation is performed, it should be for cosmetic reasons only. Speech difficulties in Down syndrome are usually due to faulty messages from the brain, and cannot be improved by an operation on the tongue.

Plastic surgery certainly has a place in the treatment of some children and adults with Down syndrome. The dangers of each operation must be known and considered. Plastic surgery should be done to improve an individual's appearance, rather than his behaviour or intellectual development.

Sensory integration therapy

This form of therapy is based on the work of Ayers, an occupational therapist, who believed that many learning problems were related to difficulties in processing incoming stimuli. The therapy consists of manoeuvres such as swinging the child, getting him to crawl, and stimulating his skin with materials of various textures. It is questionable whether such techniques influence a child's learning. Sensory integration programmes which involve activities such as spinning around and creeping may be humiliating for some children.

Massive vitamin and mineral therapy

High doses of vitamins and minerals are another treatment suggested for children with intellectual handicap. This sort of treatment is particularly advocated by those calling themselves orthomolecular physicians (or orthomolecular psychiatrists).

Although there are some rare inborn disorders that respond to certain vitamins, Down syndrome is not one of these. Trials of high doses of vitamins in children with Down syndrome have failed to show any improvement in the children treated. In fact, some vitamins can accumulate in the body and have toxic effects, slowing down the child's development and causing ill health and even death.

Orthomolecular physicians often analyse hair to obtain a 'profile' of vitamin and mineral 'deficiencies'. The levels regarded as abnormal by many of these physicians would usually be considered quite acceptable by other doctors.

'Allergy' diets and gluten-free diets

Children with Down syndrome are sometimes put on diets which exclude foods to which it is claimed they are allergic. Gluten, a protein found in wheat, rye, and oats, is a substance commonly implicated. There is no reliable evidence that children with Down syndrome improve on such diets, except for a very small number who have clear-cut allergies to a specific substance. The improvement will then be confined to allergy-related symptoms, such as hay fever, asthma, swelling, and rashes. Gluten may need to be excluded in the rare child with coeliac disease, a condition that is not associated with Down syndrome and should only be diagnosed by a paediatric gastro-enterologist (specialist in the stomach and intestines).

A diet low in phenylalanine, sometimes suggested for people with Down syndrome, has also been shown to be ineffective.

The Feingold diet

The diet suggested by the late Dr. Ben Feingold for the treatment of 'hyperactivity' consists of the exclusion of foods containing certain artificial colouring agents, as well as some naturally occurring substances present in fruits and other foods. Many controlled trials have been performed, and there is evidence that the diet may cause some improvement in overactivity, impulsivity, task-impersistence, and distractibility in a small proportion of children. When this improvement does occur, however, it is slight. The diet is difficult to keep to in its strict form, but is nutritionally sound provided care is taken to ensure that there is an adequate intake of vitamin C. Many parents report that the diet does help, and if you do feel your child improves, there is no reason why you should not keep him on the diet.

Doman–Delacato method

This is a very intensive method of treatment. It was devised at the Institute for the Achievement of Human Potential in Philadelphia and has been recommended by its originators (Glenn Doman and Carl Delacato) for many forms of disability. Similar centres now exist in other parts of the world. The Australian Centre for Brain Injured Children in Melbourne is one of these.

An individualized programme is prepared for each child, which often occupies most of the child's waking hours. A variety of manoeuvres are carried out based on the assumption that by manipulating the head and limbs (patterning), the brain will undergo 'neuronal (nerve cell) organization'. Both the theory of neuronal organization and the claims for the benefits of the treatment are open to question.

The programme is very intensive, and parents usually have to gather a circle of helpers. This is generally done by advertising in the local press. The treatment is expensive, and parents later often complain of being led to believe that it would effect a cure in their child. The heavy time-commitment of the programme may take its toll on the parents and their other children. The vigorous and continuous movement to which the helpers subject the child's body may be exhausting and painful for the child, and there is concern in some quarters that this treatment causes unnecessary suffering to the child.

Developmental optometry

Developmental optometrists believe that certain eye treatments will improve learning. These treatments include eye exercises (visual training), coloured lenses, and weak lenses to prevent eye strain (in the absence of clear-cut short- or long-sightedness). As explained earlier, the learning difficulties in children with Down syndrome are related to brain function, and it is, therefore, unlikely that these exercises would improve learning. Certainly, every child and adult with Down syndrome should have their vision regularly checked by an ophthalmologist, as outlined in Chapter 6. If vision is impaired, it may be interfering with learning, and should be treated by conventional means.

Chiropractic

Chiropractors use manipulation of the spine as a method of treating disease. This form of treatment has not been shown to help children or adults with Down syndrome. The instability of the spinal joints in some children with Down syndrome makes them vulnerable to damage to the spinal cord during spinal manipulation. Paralysis or death may follow such a procedure.

Medicines

Many substances have been tried in Down syndrome with no proven beneficial effect. Mixtures, such as the 'basis' therapy of Haubold (Germany) and the 'U-series' treatment of Turkel (United States), have been shown to be ineffective. Controlled trials have proved that dimethylsulfoxide (DMSO) and 5-hydroxytryptamine are of no benefit to children with the syndrome.

Recently, medicines that improve the hyperactivity of some children have been used in children with Down syndrome. Methylphenidate (Ritalin) and dexamphetamine (Dexedrine) are stimulants which, paradoxically, slow down some hyperactive children. The child concentrates for longer periods, persists with tasks, and is less impulsive and distractable. The medication is only effective while in the bloodstream (from approximately thirty minutes after being taken to about six hours later). Unfortunately, these medicines have been over-used in some parts of the world. They are potentially addictive, and can reduce appetite, decrease growth, and affect mood. None of these side-effects is a problem if the dose and administration of the medicine are properly controlled. The medicine improves the behaviour of some children; but research has not shown an improvement in school attainment.

A small number of children with Down syndrome have difficulty in attending to tasks and sitting still. Where these problems are out of proportion to their developmental level, such children may benefit from one of these medicines. Treatment should be under the control of a paediatrician, with feedback from the teacher and parents.

16. Future pregnancies

One of the concerns shared by many parents who have had a child with Down syndrome is whether they will have further children with the syndrome. Parents also wonder whether their other children have an increased chance of having a child with the condition.

At present, the only way of preventing Down syndrome is to detect whether an embryo or fetus has an extra chromosome 21, and if so, to terminate the pregnancy. This is a controversial subject, as some parents are strongly opposed to termination of pregnancy on ethical grounds. But surveys have shown that many parents, although they love and value their child, do not want to have another child with the condition. Fortunately, for the vast majority of such parents, the chance of having a further child with the syndrome is far less than the chance of having a normal child. Although many will choose to have a test to detect Down syndrome during pregnancy, very few will have to make the difficult decision about termination.

This chapter is written for those parents who want to calculate their chance of having another child with Down syndrome, and who want information about pre-natal tests, so that they can make an informed decision.

CALCULATING YOUR CHANCE OF HAVING ANOTHER CHILD WITH DOWN SYNDROME

The chance of having another child with Down syndrome will depend on whether your child has the common trisomy 21, a translocation, or mosaicism.

1. If your child has trisomy 21

In the case of trisomy 21, it is unnecessary for parents to have their chromosomes tested, because they cannot carry this form of Down syndrome. As mentioned in chapter 4, trisomy 21 becomes more common as the mother gets older. In calculating the chance of this occurring a second time, the first thing to look at is the mother's age. Table 2 shows the chance of a *first* child with Down syndrome being born at different maternal ages.

If a woman has already had one child with Down syndrome, there may be something special about the way in which she forms eggs, or she may be particularly efficient at carrying fetuses with an extra chromosome. These factors make the chance of a *second* child being born with Down syndrome higher than those in the table. The chance for mothers under forty who have had one child with trisomy 21 is one in a hundred, regardless of age. For mothers over the age of forty, it is probably twice as high* as it would have been had she not had a previous child with Down syndrome (see Table 6).

2. If your child has a translocation

In the case of the child having a translocation, the first thing to establish is whether one of the parents is a carrier. Table 6 summarizes the chance of having a second child with Down syndrome when the first has a translocation.

If, as occurs in the majority of cases, both parents have normal chromosomes, the probability of another child being born with Down syndrome is no higher than the usual chance for the mother's age.

If one of the parents is a carrier, it is important to establish which parent it is, and whether the chromosome on to which the number 21 is translocated is another 21 or not.

Usually the chromosome to which the translocated 21 is attached is not a number 21 (it is then a 13, 14, 15, or 22). In this case, the chance of another child with Down syndrome being born is one in eight if the mother is the carrier and one in forty if the father is the carrier. This difference occurs because men produce large numbers of sperm, and the abnormal sperm have less chance of fertilizing the egg than the normal ones. (In the case of a female carrier, only one egg is produced in each cycle, and so this particular form of competition does not occur.)

---

* This is an approximation. There are few data on women having a second child with Down syndrome after the age of forty.

Table 6. Chance of recurrence of Down syndrome

Type of Down syndrome	Parents' chromosomes	Chance of recurrence
Trisomy 21	Normal	1 in 100 if mother is under 40. If mother is over 40, twice usual chance for her age (see Table 2).
Translocation with chromosome 13, 14, 15, or 22	Normal	Usual chance for mother's age (see Table 2).
	Mother a carrier	1 in 8
	Father a carrier	1 in 40
Translocation with another chromosome 21	Normal	Usual chance for mother's age (see Table 2).
	Either parent a carrier	100%
Mosaicism	Normal	Unknown, probably the usual chance for mother's age (see Table 2).

In the extremely rare situation where the carrier parent has two 21 chromosomes joined together, the only possible outcome would be a child with Down syndrome. Such a couple could seek the advice of a genetic counsellor about alternative ways of having children, such as artificial insemination (if the father is the carrier) or egg donation (if the mother is the carrier).

Translocation carriers and other family members

If neither parent of a child with translocation Down syndrome is a carrier, the chance of any of their normal children having a child with Down syndrome is the same as for the rest of the population.

If one of the parents is a carrier, further studies of the family should be done to see whether other members are also carriers. This should be carried out under the supervision of a geneticist. Failure to do this has resulted in a number of children with Down syndrome being born to different members of the same family. This rare way in which Down syndrome 'runs' in families can be prevented by systematic testing of appropriate family members.

If any sibling or other relative is found to be a carrier, the probabilities summarized in Table 6 apply to his or her offspring. All siblings who are carriers should be informed by the time they reach adolescence about antenatal tests for Down syndrome.

3. If your child has mosaicism

If your child has mosaicism, your chance of having further children with the syndrome is likely to be lower than if your child had ordinary trisomy 21. Mosaicism is rare, and there are insufficient data for a precise numerical probability to be calculated.

TESTS DURING PREGNANCY

Tests to detect Down syndrome in future pregnancies provide what is referred to as 'antenatal diagnosis of Down syndrome', that is, the detection of Down syndrome in the fetus.

Knowing the chance of having another child with Down syndrome helps you make up your mind whether to go ahead with such a test. But it is not simply a matter of comparing one statistic with another, that is to say the statistical chance of having a child with Down syndrome versus the statistical chance of miscarriage (the main complication of the tests). You will also need to weigh up your *feelings* about a second child with Down syndrome in your family against your *feelings* about a miscarriage.

Parents who request antenatal diagnosis are sometimes asked whether they would agree to termination if the test was found to be positive. Most couples find it difficult to predict what they would do while the chance of the fetus having Down syndrome is merely theoretical.

You should feel free to have the test, even if you are not sure what you would do in the case of an abnormal result. In most cases you will not have to deliberate, because the result will be normal. If it is abnormal, a decision can then be made.

The tests available to detect Down syndrome during pregnancy are amniocentesis and chorionic villi biopsy.

1. Amniocentesis

The commonest form of antenatal diagnosis for Down syndrome is amniocentesis. This is a test which has been performed for many years all over the world. On account of the expense involved, governments will usually only make this service available to couples with a relatively high chance of having a child with Down syndrome. This means mothers of advanced maternal age (usually over thirty-five or thirty-seven years, depending on the country or state), or in cases where a previous child has been born with Down syndrome. Another reason for having the test is when the mother is unusually anxious about having an abnormal child. The decision is usually left to the doctor's discretion.

Amniocentesis is generally performed by obstetricians experienced in this procedure. At each major centre there are often only one or two obstetricians who perform this test. In this way they become very adept at it. This means that, even though you may have an obstetrician of your own, it may be necessary for him or her to arrange for another obstetrician to carry out this procedure.

The test is a simple one, and is performed at an outpatients' clinic. It is carried out between the sixteenth and eighteenth week of pregnancy (counted from the date of the beginning of the last menstrual period). The pregnant woman will be given instructions to drink extra amounts of fluid, and not to pass urine for a few hours prior to the procedure. This is because a full bladder allows good visualization of the womb during the preliminary ultra-sound scan.

The woman lies on her back, and initially an ultra-sound examination is performed, so that the position of the fetus and the placenta can be seen. The ultra-sound scan is performed by sliding an instrument (transducer) lubricated with jelly over the front of the abdomen. Once this is done, the woman can empty her bladder, and the obstetrician will insert a very thin needle

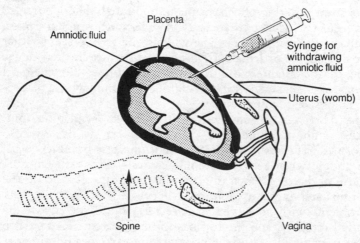

Fig. 23. Amniocentesis.

through the front of the abdomen just below the navel (Fig. 23). Some obstetricians inject a small amount of local anaesthetic prior to this. If not, the woman will feel the needle go through the skin as if it were a pin-prick. No further pain is experienced as the needle passes further through the abdomen towards the womb. Once the needle enters the womb, the obstetrician lets it continue for a short distance, until the end is in the sac of amniotic fluid that surrounds the baby. A small amount of this fluid is withdrawn into a syringe, and it is this that is sent to the laboratory for the test. The fluid is usually straw-coloured, owing to the presence of protein and certain other substances. The needle is then withdrawn, and the tiny hole that it has made is obliterated by the natural elasticity of the tissues. The woman is encouraged to rest for a short while after the procedure, usually half an hour or so, and can then go home. For the rest of that day she should avoid vigorous activity.

The fluid that has been taken has, suspended within it, cells shed from the skin of the fetus in the normal course of events. In the laboratory, these skin cells are placed in special fluid and kept at a warm temperature, so that they can divide and grow. When there are enough cells they can be harvested, and their chromosomes can be extracted and stained. This allows them to be seen under the microscope and counted. The laboratory technician (cytogeneticist) can then determine whether Down syndrome is present. He or she will also be able to see whether the child is male or female, by looking at the sex chromosomes. Some of the amniotic fluid can be sent off to do chemical testing for a substance called alpha-fetoprotein, which, if present in raised quantities, may suggest that the fetus has spina bifida. This has nothing to do with Down syndrome; but, because amniotic fluid is available, this test is usually also performed. The result of the chromosome test becomes available about two weeks after amniocentesis. This delay occurs because of the time taken to grow the cells, as well as to do the laborious staining and counting.

Problems with amniocentesis are rare. Now and again, the cells fail to grow, and the test has to be repeated. The test also causes a slight increase in the risk of miscarriage. If this does happen after amniocentesis, it usually occurs two to three weeks after the event. The risk of miscarriage occurring after amniocentesis is about one in a hundred.

2. Chorionic villi biopsy

Another, newer alternative to amniocentesis is chorionic villi biopsy (CVB), also known as chorionic villi sampling (CVS). This test, which has become increasingly available over the past few years, has the advantage of being performed much earlier in pregnancy. It can be done from six weeks after the date of the last menstrual period, although the ideal time is between the ninth and eleventh week of pregnancy. It is performed at an outpatients' clinic, and is usually carried out only by certain obstetricians.

In this test a very thin, flexible tube is inserted up the vagina and into the lower end of the womb (Fig. 24). The woman lies on her back, and the procedure is associated with the same kind of discomfort as is experienced when a Pap smear is performed. An ultra-sound scan is done at the same time, so that the passage of the tube can be seen. The end of the tube is used to suck up the chorionic villi, small, finger-like projections of the primitive placenta. The flexible tube is then removed, and the fetal tissue is sent to the laboratory. At the laboratory, the cells of the villi are grown, and their chromosomes are extracted and stained and looked at under the microscope.

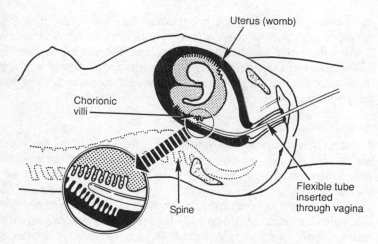

Uterus (womb)

Chorionic villi

Flexible tube inserted through vagina

Spine

Fig. 24. Chorionic villi biopsy.

Chorionic villi are made up of special rapidly dividing cells, which grow to become the placenta. Growth of these cells in the laboratory is therefore extremely quick, and it is possible for the chromosome result to be available a day or two after the procedure. In practice, many laboratories grow the cells for longer, because this allows details on individual chromosomes to be seen with greater consistency. You may therefore have to wait about two weeks before getting the results in many centres.

The alpha-fetoprotein test, mentioned with amniocentesis, cannot be performed on chorionic villi. This substance can only be measured in the amniotic fluid or in blood.

Chorionic villi biopsy is a relatively new procedure, and is not always available. In some centres, parents will be given a choice of chorionic villi biopsy or amniocentesis. Although chorionic villi biopsy has a higher risk of being followed by a miscarriage than amniocentesis, it should be remembered that it is performed earlier in the pregnancy, when the risk of a spontaneous miscarriage is higher. Chorionic villi biopsy increases the usual risk at nine weeks (approximately two in a hundred) to somewhere between three and four in a hundred.

As with amniocentesis, there is always a small chance that the cells will not grow, and that the procedure will have to be repeated. This is less of a problem with chorionic villi biopsy,

as the pregnancy has not progressed very far when it is performed, and there is consequently more time to repeat the test.

An increasing number of couples are choosing chorionic villi
biopsy, rather than amniocentesis, because of the earlier results.
This makes termination, if needed, easier both medically and
psychologically.

Twin pregnancies

If twins are identical and one has Down syndrome, the other
will also have the condition. If one of a non-identical pair has
the syndrome, the other is likely to be normal. In the case of a
woman carrying twins, both amniocentesis and chorionic villi
biopsy can still be performed, although they do become more
difficult. Samples of fluid or villi must be taken from both
fetuses, and each sample tested separately. It is possible to
terminate the fetus with Down syndrome, while allowing the
unaffected fetus to continue.

When the result becomes available

In the majority of cases, the result of amniocentesis or chorionic villi sampling will be normal.

If the test reveals that the fetus has Down syndrome, the
parents will need to make a decision about whether they want
to terminate the pregnancy. It is often worth while for parents
to talk to a social worker experienced in this area, who can help
them come to a decision.

Whatever counselling parents receive, the decision should
always be their own. If termination is requested, this is performed by admitting the pregnant woman to hospital and giving her medication, usually through a drip, to start the womb
contracting so that the contents are expelled. Sometimes an
operation is needed to empty the womb.

What a 'normal' result means

When the result of the amniocentesis or the chorionic villi
biopsy shows that the child has normal chromosomes, this
means that neither Down syndrome nor any other major chromosomal abnormality is present. The ultra-sound scan which is
performed together with these procedures is also able to ex-

clude certain malformations. This does not give a 100 per cent assurance that the child is going to be normal. There are a number of conditions that could still be present. But parents can feel reassured that these are not more common in families where one of the children has Down syndrome.

SCREENING TESTS

Only amniocentesis and chorionic villi biopsy can establish with certainty whether a fetus has Down syndrome. For women who have had a previous child with Down syndrome, or are in the older age group, these tests are appropriate.

Two-thirds of children with Down syndrome are born to younger mothers, who have not had a previous child with the syndrome. There has therefore been a great impetus to find a simple blood test which could be offered to younger pregnant women, and that would detect those who are more likely to be carrying a fetus with the syndrome. Such a test would allow routine screening of all pregnant women, with definitive tests (amniocentesis or chorionic villi biopsy) provided to those with an abnormal result. In this way, a greater number of fetuses with Down syndrome would be detected without the need for many more women to have an amniocentesis.

Since 1984, a number of screening tests have been developed, and routine testing of all pregnant women may be introduced in some countries over the next few years. These tests are based on the discovery that the maternal blood level of certain substances* normally produced by the fetus (and placenta) are often altered when the fetus has Down syndrome. Measurement of these substances does not become reliable until after the sixteenth week of pregnancy, so that if definitive testing is indicated, amniocentesis rather than chorionic villi biopsy will have to be performed.

It must be emphasized that the measurement of these substances only indicates that there is a greater possibility that the fetus has Down syndrome. A proportion of women who are carrying fetuses with Down syndrome will have normal levels of these substances, while some women with normal fetuses will have abnormal levels.

---

* Lowered alpha-fetoprotein (raised in spina bifida), lowered unconjugated oestriol, and raised human chorionic gonadotrophin.

Conclusion

There has been a profound change in attitude to individuals with Down syndrome over the past two decades. Indeed, it has been one of the most positive social changes of this century. What has been the origin of this change?

Some have suggested that it has been due to changes in government policy; others have attributed the change to the originators of normalization theory. But this change would not have occurred had it not been for parents and their faith in their children.

More and more parents have decided to rear their children with Down syndrome at home, often against professional advice and with little in the way of support. They have brought up their children as part of the family, providing them with a caring and stimulating environment in which to grow and learn. They have formed associations to support one another, and to stimulate professionals to take a new look at the syndrome. They have demanded greater opportunities for education, recreation, and employment. One need only attend a parent group meeting, an early intervention session, or a conference held by a Down syndrome association, to be struck by parents' eagerness to help their children, their desire to learn more about the condition, and their obvious pride in their children's achievements.

The change in parental attitude has, in turn, resulted in the increased competence of individuals with Down syndrome. Today, people with the syndrome are healthier, more capable, and more integrated into the community than ever before. As a result, other members of the community have a greater awareness of their individuality and potential.

With these developments, the future for people with Down syndrome looks brighter than ever, and holds the promise of greater opportunities and greater fulfilment.

Appendix: Useful addresses

UNITED KINGDOM

Down's Syndrome Association, 12–13 Clapham Common South Side, London SW4 7AA.
MENCAP (Royal Society for Mentally Handicapped Children and Adults), 123 Golden Lane, London EC1 ORT.
Voluntary Council for Handicapped Children, 8 Wakley Street, London EC1V 7QE.
Advocacy Alliance, 115 Golden Lane, London EC1.
British Institute of Mental Handicap, Wolverhampton Road, Kidderminster. Worcestershire DY10 3PP.

UNITED STATES OF AMERICA

National Down Syndrome Congress, 1800 Dempster Street, Park Ridge, IL 60068.
National Down Syndrome Society, 141 Fifth Avenue, New York, NY 10010.

AUSTRALIA

Australian Down Syndrome Association, 91 Hutt Street, Adelaide 5000.
This is the national association. In addition, each state has an active association of its own.

CANADA

Down's Syndrome Association of Metropolitan Toronto, 20 Barkwood Crescent, Willowdale, Ontario M2H3G6.

NEW ZEALAND

N.Z. Down's Syndrome Association, PO Box 4142, Auckland 1.

IRELAND

Down's Syndrome Association of Ireland, 27 South William Street, Dublin 2.

SOUTH AFRICA

Down's Syndrome Association (Tvl), 87 Waterfall Avenue, Craighall 2024.

Index

activity therapy centres 168–9
adenoids, *see* glue ear
adolescence 146–57
adult education, *see* further education
adulthood 158–97
advocacy 161–2
Advocacy Alliance 162, 199
after-school care 113
ageing 176–9
allergies 184
Alzheimer disease 177–8, 182
amniocentesis 192–4
antenatal diagnosis 191–7
assessments 115–24, 133–4
    definition of 115
    timing of 118–19
atlanto-axial instability 70, 79–81,
    175–6
atrio-ventricular canal (AV canal) 90
atrio-ventricular septal defect 89–91
    complete 90–1
    partial 90

basis therapy 186
behaviour 96–107
    modification of 96–103
biting 106
blood tests 71
body odour, *see* puberty
bones 78
brachycephaly 30
breast feeding 50
brief restraint 100
British Institute of Mental Handicap
    199
Brushfield spots 30–1

care co-ordinator 108–9, 163
carriers 41–2, 189–91
cataracts 77–8
cells 33, 34
cell therapy 181–2
chewing 59
child development centres 109, 116–17

children of people with Down
    syndrome 172–3
chiropractic 186
chorionic villi biopsy 194–6
chromosomal error in Down syndrome
    35
chromosome number 21
    Down syndrome region on 35, 36
chromosomes 33, 34
circles of social distance 155
citizen advocacy 161–2
classes
    ordinary 139–41
    pre-school 135–6
    special 141–2
classification of Down syndrome 35–6,
    37
clinodactyly 31
clothes 65, 153, 159
coffee clubs, *see* social development in
    adolescence
cognitive development 47, 52, 56, 62,
    64–5
colds, *see* upper respiratory tract
    infections
Commonwealth Employment Service
    167
communication book 137–8
community living centres 165
community mental handicap team 109
community services for the
    developmentally disabled 109
constipation 86–7
contraception 173–5
controlled crying 101
controlled trials 180–1
coping
    during the new-born period 7–12
    with the reactions of others 24–5
crawling 53–4
crèches 134
crossed-eyes, *see* squint

day nurseries 134

definition-by-use 55
dental checks 71
destructive behaviour 107
development
areas of 46–7
major milestones of 49
maximum potential for 45
rate of 43–4
review of 47–60
stops and starts in 45–6
developmental achievement centres 165
developmental age 121
developmental checklist 131, 133
developmental disability 122
developmental optometry 185–6
developmental tests 119–24
dexamphetamine (Dexedrine) 186–7
diabetes 179
diagnosis of Down syndrome 29
diet
Feingold 184–5
gluten-free 184
weight control 149
dietitian 149
dimethylsulfoxide (DMSO) 186
disability
telling your child about his or her 156–7
discos, see social development in adolescence
district handicap teams 109, 117
doctor 9, 103, 108, 176
Doman-Delacato method 185
domestic mimicry 58
double-jointed 78
Down, Dr J.L. 27
Down syndrome associations 110, 199–200
dribbling 104
duodenal atresia 85–6

early intervention
centre-based 130
definition of 125–6
effect on child of 126–7
effect on parents of 127–8
home-based 130
ears
glue ear 70, 73–5
infection of 72–3
Education Act (1981) 116
educational placement
choosing an 138–9
options 139–44
reviews of 145
Education Department
assessments by 116
education for adults, see further education
Eisenmenger complex 92–3
employment 166–9
open 167
sheltered 167–8
endocardial cushion defect 90
endocarditis 95
epicanthic fold 30
epilepsy 178
extinction 101
eyes 30–1, 75–8

face 30
features, characteristic of Down syndrome 29–32
feet 31–2, 78
fertility 172–3
financial assistance 113–14
fine-motor development 46, 48, 51, 54–5, 58, 61, 64
fingers 31
5-hydroxytryptamine 186
flat feet 78
friends 23–4, 65–6, 110, 112, 169
further education 165–6

Gateway clubs 170
genes 33
geneticist 19, 191
glasses 75, 76
glue ear 70, 73–5
grandparents 22–3
gross-motor development 46, 48, 49, 51, 53–4, 57–8, 61, 64
group homes 163–4
guardians 160–1

hair 31
half-way houses 163–4
hands 31
Hashimoto thyroiditis 84–5
head 30
health
checks 67–71, 175–6
maintenance 67–71, 175–6
hearing
loss 75
tests 70

hearing-aids 75
heart
  normal 88–9
  disorders of 89–95
height 32
Hirschsprung disease 86, 87
historical background 27
hitting 106
hobbies 113, 170
home help services 109
host families 111
hyperactivity 58, 104–5, 184–5, 186–7
hypothyroidism 83–5
  acquired 84–5
  congenital 83–4
hypotonia 32, 78
hysterectomy 175

immune system 179
immunizations 71
incidence 28, 39
individual education programmes 145
individual programme planning 162–3
Institute for the Achievement of
    Human Potential 185
institutions 163–4
intellect
  disability in 122–4
  impairment of 122, 123
intelligence quotient (IQ)
  definition of 121
  ranges 121–4
intelligence tests 119–24
intestines 85–7

joints 78

keratoconus 78
key worker 108–9, 163
kindergarten 134
Klinefelter syndrome 87

language development 46–7, 50, 52,
    55–6, 59–60, 62, 64
lazy eye 76
legal assistance 114
legal control 160–1
leisure
  for adolescents, see social
    development
  for adults 169–70
  for children, see recreation
leisure buddy schemes 112, 169–70

leukaemia 87
long-sightedness 75
loss, preparation for 157

Makaton 60
Manpower Services Commission 167
marriage
  adults with Down syndrome and
    171–2
  effect of having a child with Down
    syndrome on 13–16
marriage guidance 15
masturbation 152–3
maternal age 28, 37, 38, 39
MENCAP 167, 170, 199
menstruation 147–8, 150, 151–2
mental age 121, 159
mental handicap 122
mental retardation 122
methylphenidate (Ritalin) 186–7
middle ear infections, see ears
minerals 184
mosaicism 42
  chance of recurrence of 191
mouth 31
muscle tone 32, 78

National Down Syndrome Congress
    199
National Down Syndrome Society 199
neck 31, 79, see also atlanto-axial
    instability
neuronal organization 185
non-disjunction 36
normalization 159–60
nucleus 33, 34
nursery school 134
nystagmus 77

obesity 148–50
occupational therapist 128–9
Office of Intellectual Disability 109
orthomolecular physicians 184
ostium primum defect 90
overactivity 104–5, see also
    hyperactivity

paediatrician 108, 118
palmar crease 31, 32
parent and child groups 134
parents' reactions 4–7
patent ductus arteriosus 92
paternal age 38–9
Pathway scheme 167

patterning 185
personal development 46, 48, 49, 50, 52,
    55, 58–9, 61–2, 64
physical examinations
    new-born 68–9
    routine 70–1
physiotherapist 128
plastic surgery 182–3
pregnancy in women with Down
    syndrome 172
prenatal tests, see antenatal diagnosis
pre-school 134
    groups 62, 134–6
prevalence 28
programme officer 103
psychologist 103, 117–18
puberty
    body odour during 150
    clumsiness during 148
    early changes of 146–7
    in boys 147
    increased appetite during 148–50
    in girls 147–8
    mood changes during 148
Public Law (94–142) 116

recognition of Down syndrome 29
recreation
    for adolescents, see social
        development
    for adults, see leisure
    for children 112–13
recreation newsletter 112
recreation officer 112
referential looking 56
relatives 23–4
reports 120
respite-care 103, 110–11
review of development 47–60
    the first year 51–3
    the new-born 48, 50, 51
    the pre-schooler 60–3
    the school-aged child 63–6
    the second year 53–7
    the toddler 57–60
rewards 98, 102
runny nose, see upper respiratory tract
    infections

salivary glands 104
school holiday care 113
schools
    ordinary 139–41

private 144–5
    residential 144
    special 136, 142–4
school transport 145
screening tests for Down syndrome 197
seizures 178–9
self-advocacy 161–2
sensory integration therapy 183–4
services, guide to 108–14
sex education 151
sexual abuse 154–5
sexuality
    adolescent 147–8, 151–3
    adult 170–1
short-sightedness 76
siblings 16–22
    books for 21
    groups for 21
    responsibilities of 19
    special time with 19
    teasing of 20–2
    telling about Down syndrome 17–19
    younger 20
sicca cell therapy, see cell therapy
sign and say 60
single parents 16
skin 81–2
social development 46, 48, 49, 50, 52,
    55, 58–9, 61–2, 64
    in adolescence 153
social education centres 169
social worker 9, 118, 196
special educator 129
sporting activities 112
squint 30, 76–7
sterilization 174–5
stranger anxiety 55
syndrome 26

talking, see language development
tantrums 58–9, 96, 106
teeth 82–3, 95
telling about Down syndrome
    child with Down syndrome 156–7
    grandparents 22
    parents 2–3
    relatives and friends 23
    siblings 17–9
temperament 26, see also behaviour
terminology 27
terrible twos 58–9
tetralogy of Fallot 94–5
thioridazine (Melleril) 153